261.2
G37
a
    Gilbert, Arthur, rabbi.
       A Jew in Christian
    America.

A JEW IN CHRISTIAN AMERICA

A JEW
in Christian America

RABBI ARTHUR GILBERT

SHEED AND WARD : NEW YORK

© *Sheed and Ward, Inc., 1966*

Library of Congress Catalog Card Number: 66-12272

Manufactured in the United States of America

Contents

Preface

THIS PAST THANKSGIVING I spent a most unusual weekend. On one evening I visited a Catholic theological seminary in the Midwest in order to discuss with the faculty the ways by which we could help their students acquire a profounder understanding of the nature of Jews and Judaism; and I was given the Bishop's Suite as my lodging place for the night. The next day I addressed a national, college-age, Lutheran convention and I was housed in the Martin Luther Room in the bell tower of the Seminary's magnificent church. That Friday evening Protestant students viewed a Jewish Sabbath service and then at their suggestion we all danced the Horah—the national folk dance of the State of Israel—around the statue of Martin Luther. We sang out loudly in the Hebrew: "Who Are We?—Israel."

Such an ecumenical experience was not really without precedent for me. It has been my work since 1953 to represent the concerns of the Jewish community before Protestant and Catholic leaders and to foster, as best as I could, inter-religious understanding. Yet I never do get over the feeling of surprise and delightful unexpectedness at such encounters. Each interreligious experience seems to me a new one, like the spirit-renewing reacquaintance of brothers long separated from each other. It is not insignificant that the Christian teen-agers and I could both sing out lustily "We Are Israel," for at the depths this is exactly what we do share together: a sense of ourselves as being covenanted in community to God and obliged by faith to witness to Him and to serve our fellow man in love and justice.

The truth is, also, despite our kinship to the one Father, that Jews and Christians have been separated from each other in bitterness over long centuries. We are only now rediscovering each other in our authentic existences.

Perhaps my sense of unexpectancy is related also to the fact that I have not yet fully worked out for myself all the harsh memories of the times past when Jews feared and hated Christians. Thus I find a catharsis, a renewal of self in encounters of understanding with my Christian neighbor.

In each confrontation with Christianity I am forced back to my own roots, each time with a new perspective gained from the sharing of the truths nurtured by the Christian. Thus I find myself enriched and enriching my Judaism. I like to think that when Jews and Christians define themselves to each other, they are each adding to the other's vision of the Divine.

My vocation has not always been easy. Stimulated by what appeared to be an opening particularly in Protestant ranks following World War II, the Anti-Defamation League employed a rabbi to work full time among Christian educators and social action executives. There was but one other rabbi then engaged in such work in the United States. Cooperatively he and I "divided" the entire Christian community between ourselves. Despite knowledge of the anguish of Jews in the crematoria and the soul-searching undertaken by many Christians—how could such brutality have erupted in a Christian influenced culture?—there were many doors still closed to us. Catholics, for example, were imprisoned behind their own ghetto walls. Priests were unavailable for interreligious dialogue. The administrators of Catholic schools, colleges, and seminaries never dreamed of having their students visit the synagogue or of inviting a rabbi to visit them. Catholic publishers were hesitant about including textbook materials describing the contemporary beliefs and practices of Jews.

Nevertheless, we worked hard at creating occasions. We sought out those in the church who were ready to pioneer the way and we made fellowship with them. We started wherever we could in each denomination, mostly with the executives of youth programming; then we moved on from one age-group department to the next, from one denomination or religious order to the next. In time I had the unusual pleasure of being able to introduce a Southern Baptist educator to a Unitarian, both of whom were attending as observers a National Council of Churches Conference, or a Jesuit theologian to a Benedictine historian. I like to feel that in some small way I was a "secret weapon" in the ecumenical movement.

In truth, there were many larger pressures and tendencies, challenges from without the church and stirrings from within, that erupted into a glorious display of an interreligious seeking after each other, a healthy contentiousness over issues in the public order such as religious practices in public education and federal funds for church-related schools, a readiness for the first time to talk honestly to each other without the false grin of the Brotherhood Week mask.

One of the first things we discovered was that we really had no clear idea of the other. Our response to each other had been in terms of our own distorted conceptions. Sensitive and concerned Christians asked Jews to tell them something of their history. Who are the Jews? What has been their experience in the Christian world? What has been God's dealings with Jews since Jesus emerged from their midst? It was in response to questions such as these, at the invitation of Protestant and Catholic editors, that most of the chapters in this book originally had been written.

I deem it an honor and a pleasure, and an evidence itself of the ongoing effort to be informed, that a Catholic publishing house has chosen to collect these essays into a book.

Not all of the essays are reprinted from Christian publications. Jews, too, were curious about Christians and I was invited by many Jewish periodicals to interpret events in the Christian community. A sampling of such essays is also to be found here.

As a result of participation in the dialogue many of my attitudes and judgments on issues in conflict between Jews and Christians were modified. For example, I came to believe that the rigidity (a loaded word, I realize), of the Jewish position on church-state matters was in great measure an understandably defensive posture arising from past memories of Christian church-statism rather than deriving from an intrinsic requirement of Jewish faith. Seeking a modification in the Jewish position I wrote many articles on the subject. Once, in answer to such a piece, a rabbi entitled his article "Battle Fatigue—A Reply to Rabbi Arthur Gilbert." He contended that I had become weary from holding the banners in the front lines of the Jewish-Christian conflict on church-state issues. What the rabbi failed to realize, of course, was that those who engaged in the interreligious dialogue all change in some way. Our confrontation is not like that of soldiers embattled with each other, but rather it is more like that of confused pilgrims quarreling with each other over the way they ought to go in order, more efficiently, to arrive at the very same destination.

It is exactly the fear of any change in religious outlook or political stance that leads conservatives in all faith communities, Catholic, Protestant, and Jewish, to suspect the ecumenical movement. This is unfortunate, because in my view such persons cut themselves off from the voice of God. I believe that God speaks to man through the history and experiences of the other. I have found that the interreligious conversation has both deepened me in my difference yet has broadened me in my ability to accept another's uniqueness. It seems to me that the issue is not who holds truth and who is in error, but rather it is a question of understanding how God's revelation could have worked itself out differently in the style of life and experiences of each other's faith. Thus the Word has meaning for me both in the particularistic form in which I cherish it, as well as in its universalistic significance through which I come to experience the existence of the other as my brother.

It is no accident, therefore, that most of these essays are popular history. They were an attempt to gather the salient facts of life so that the reader of periodicals could easily acquire essential information about his neighbor. It would be better, of course, were each of us to read the scholarly histories of the other. Hopefully, in fact, there will be just enough in this book to inspire some interested readers to turn to Heinrich Graetz's six volumes and to Solomon Grayzel's works, and to those of Abraham Sacher and Rufus Learsi, to all of whom I am indebted for much of the information the reader will find here. No effort was made to footnote my quotations and data. These are available either in the originally published manuscripts or in the historic literature to which I make reference. What is novel in my work is not the research into original sources but rather the audience to which this material is directed and the viewpoint that shaped the particular selection of facts.

It takes time and experience for a viewpoint to develop in depth. I am satisfied that in selecting these particular essays, most of which are of recent vintage, Sheed and Ward's editor, Mr. Philip Scharper, has exercised a wise and mature discretion. Much of my earlier writings are a prelude to statements I make here. I have no doubt that in another ten years, God willing, I will want to say it all over again differently. The chances are, too, that hardly any single reader of this book will have read all of the wide ranging religious periodicals in which these essays first appeared, and so I hope there will be something new and provocative for each reader.

"The Gentiles in My Life" (Chapter 1), was written originally for the International Journal of Religious Education, May 1964, an official publication of the Division of Christian Education in the National Council of Churches.

The editors wanted their Protestant readers, teachers and Church school administrators, to know something of how it might feel to grow up as a minority group child in a Christian dominated world. I tried as best I could to recapture some of the fun and pain of my childhood in Philadelphia. I had lived in a neighborhood that was largely Catholic and Jewish contiguous to a German Protestant community at the time of the shocking growth of the Nazi German-American Bund. This essay was the most popular I have ever written. It was reprinted in at least four other denominational magazines for high school and college-age youth.

Two of these essays were commissioned by Presbyterian Life, Chapter 3 "Anti-Semitism in the United States," and Chapter 9 "Theological Issues in Jewish-Christian Relations." The first was published in January 1966; unfortunately the press of other internal church problems delayed the publication of the second. Thus, it appears in this book. The essay on anti-Semitism evoked the most mail that I had ever received for one of my articles—zealous friends of the John Birch Society rose to the occasion of my passing reference to the organization and deluged me with an abuse that only verified for me my convictions about their extremism. They are hereby warned that I am immune from such harassment.

"A Short History of the Relations Between Jews and Christians" (Chapter 2), and "Reform Judaism in the United States 1890–1965" (Chapter 4), were both written for Jewish periodicals. The Christian reader is given a chance here to peek into the effort made inside the Jewish community to discuss the significance of our experiences and to chart a course for ourselves in the Christian world. The first of these was written for Jewish teen-agers. It is included in a religious school textbook entitled *Currents and Trends in Contemporary Jewish Thought*, Ktav Publishing House, 1965. The second was written on the occasion of the 75th anniversary of the founding of the Central Conference of American Rabbis. It is an appreciation of the impact of America on Reform Judaism and a critique of our own contribution to American life. Undoubtedly, the Christian reader will find that much of the experience of change within his own religious group has not been far different from that experienced by Jews. The essay, as it appears here, is in its original length. It had to be cut drastically in order to fit into the page requirements of the distinguished scholarly Jewish magazine Judaism, Fall 1965. I'm delighted, therefore, at this chance for the publication of the fuller discourse.

Chapters 5, 6, and 7 are articles that were written during my four-year responsibility as Director of the National Conference of Christians and Jews Ford Foundation-financed project, Religious Freedom and Public Affairs. This project was intended to encourage clergy and lay dialogue across faith lines on issues of religious freedom. In Chapter 5, "Legislation, Litigation, Dialogue—Methods Used to Achieve Religious Freedom in the United States," I tried to describe how the emergent religious pluralism determined the methods employed in changing the prevailing status quo arrangements as well as the direction of that change. The article appeared as a chapter in the book *Religion and the Public Order 1964*, a publication of the Institute of Church and State of the Villanova University School of Law. It was published by the University of Chicago Press, 1965.

"The Education Act of 1965 and American Jewry" (Chapter 6), is an analysis of the divisions within the Jewish community over the use of public funds in assistance to children attending church-related schools. The reader will note throughout my own strong convictions that the "Johnson consensus" on this issue is not at all a threat to American religious liberty. To the contrary, I believe it will enhance religious freedom. It is, itself, a fruit of the growth of the interreligious trust in the United States. This essay was published by the CCAR Journal of the Central Conference of American Rabbis, October 1965, as part of a debate on policy to be enacted by Reform rabbis.

"Religious Pluralism—A Jewish View" (Chapter 7), was

published in Theology Today, January 1963, the organ of the Princeton Theological School. In this essay I try first to provide a theological perspective on Jewish attitudes towards religious pluralism, and then to raise in a sociological way the problems all religions must confront as they differ with each other as shapers and formers of American public morality. In this bi-faceted approach to religious pluralism I demonstrate my conviction that theology undergirds the conviction that each of us brings into the public order. In resolving differences on matters of public policy, however, we are required to consider the common good in its secular dimension and to remain sensitive to the rights of others in good conscience to hold to differing value judgments. Religious leaders must be wary of imposing a sectarian morality upon society through the wielding of political power in the legislation of law.

Two fine hours in my life are recalled by the inclusion in this book of an address delivered before the World Congress of the Catholic Press in New York in May 1965 (Chapter 8), and a talk delivered to the Lutheran World Federation's consultation on The Church and the Jewish People at the Logumkloster, Denmark, in May of 1964 (Chapter 10). I am certain that the invitations extended to me on those occasions have a significance far beyond my own personal involvement. For this reason, therefore, I carry with me to this day a profound sense of the inadequacy of my word: The opportunities were beyond my ability and the enthusiasm of the response was related only in a small measure to my achievement.

The Lutherans were reconsidering in all earnestness their theological stance with regard to the Jews. By virtue of the legacy of Martin Luther's hostility toward Jews and the complicity of German Lutheranism in Nazi anti-Semitism, this meeting was charged with historic verve. As part of their deliberation, the Lutherans wanted a Jew to define his own conception of the Jewish mission in history. They welcomed, also, a Jewish reaction to their conversations. But the Lutherans, no less than I, were uncertain as to whether we could speak our minds to each other and yet not offend. Is it possible to believe earnestly in the particular redemptive significance of one's own revelation and yet not denigrate a dispensation that differs?

The paradox in all this is that the German theologians were most creatively radical in their understandings of the church's relation to the Jew; and I was drawn closer to them in a way that I would never have thought possible. These Germans were not only reacting out of a sense of guilt for past offense, but their painful awareness of their own infidelity to God's word of love humbled them and they appreciated how much fidelity to God there had been in the Jew's adherence to Judaism despite persecution. Having experienced the anguish of the Jews they rejected any tendency to dehumanize us by impersonalized, romanticized theologizing. Seeking a confrontation with the Jew in his humanity, in his Jewishness, they were ready to listen to us as we are, rather than as defined by Christian expectations.

The burden I carried as a lone Jewish spokesman was too heavy and I confessed my inadequacy. No Jew can speak for all others. The distinctiveness of God's covenant with the Jew is that He has related himself to us as a community. When next Lutherans open themselves to conversation on this issue I am certain they will invite many Jews with a wide variety of viewpoints.

The invitation to the World Congress of the Catholic Press was also a signal moment in my life. To begin with, I was to share the platform with Reverend John Courtney Murray S.J., heroic architect of the Church's position on religious liberty. Secondly, I interpreted the invitation to me as an occasion to comment frankly on the deliberations, then still taking place in Rome, on the Church's attitude toward the Jews. Finally, I was aware that editors of Catholic newspapers from every part of the world were present. The invitation to a rabbi to address them was not without its reconciling and pioneering aspects.

There was really no doubt in my mind, despite the cautious tone of my text, that the Catholic Church eventually would denounce vigorously any form of anti-Semitism. I was assured also that the Council would reject any Scriptural view of the Jews as an accursed or rejected people, and eschew the suggestion that the Jews are collectively responsible for the crucifixion. But I remained uncertain as to whether the Church would know how to view the Jews in their contemporaneous existence. Granted that the Jews are dear to God "for the sake of the fathers," but what is the meaning and significance of Jewish history since Jesus appeared in our midst? What lessons can the Church learn from the ongoingness of God's relation to the Jews? It was to such a consideration that I was really directing my remarks. I was setting forth the agenda, as it were, for future dialogues and consultations between Jews and Christians.

It is to such an ongoing rediscovery of each other that I offer this book, grateful to colleagues, Jewish and Christian, who provided inspiration and urged me on at the most difficult moments.

A JEW IN CHRISTIAN AMERICA

1

The Gentiles in My Life

THE FIRST TIME I realized that others were different and that not everyone was Jewish was when I was four years old. After an exhausting game of "run around the block," my best boyfriend and neighbor, Timmie McGrath, and I together relieved ourselves by the backyard drainpipe. The difference between us, of course, was quite obvious.

There were to be other differences. I loved Timmie better than my brother, and just wouldn't accept the fact that he couldn't go to the same public school as I did. We gradually drifted apart.

What made the separation even more difficult was my awareness that Timmie went to "church"—a strange and forbidding building that was right next to the plot on which my synagogue stood. I noticed, too, that the priest and rabbi, when passing each other on the street, never nodded or seemed to recognize each other. This troubled me, because I fantasized that both of them, being men of God, must have known each other. I suspected that they shared a closeness to God which, in truth, I envied. I used to think of God as a kind teacher who gave clergymen assignments; so certainly they must have known about each other's responsibilities.

But there was more to it than that. My grandfather used to spit when he passed the church. He explained that "they" were murderers who had killed Jews.

My mother used to tell a story which, for some reason, we children loved to hear over and over. When she was a girl, she explained, she once stood in front of a church, with her blue and white coin box, collecting money for the Jewish National Fund.

Well, one day, a man said to her: "What are you collecting for, little girl?"

She answered: "If we have enough money we can buy land in Palestine and go there to live."

He gave her a five-dollar bill. How I wished someone would put five dollars in *my* box. Even if "they" wanted to get rid of us, the joke was on them. Five dollars! Wow!

My impression that Roman Catholics hated Jews was most dramatically clarified for me when the boys from the neighborhood "R.C. Church" goose-stepped in front of our synagogue during Yom Kippur, the Jewish Day of Atonement. Our parents prayed all day inside, and restless children played part of the time outside. The Catholic boys shouted, "Heil Hitler," obviously taunting us. In fact, I first learned the significance of that tyrant from their taunts. It was a victory to fight them off on Yom Kippur.

But to confuse the issue, the neighbor on the other side of our house was also a Catholic. Mrs. Strahan was my favorite "aunt." Her son was studying to be a priest. I found it hard to believe. He was such a nice man.

When I got to junior high school, the growth of Nazism had become even more serious. There was a heavy German-American population across the way, and the Nazis used to pick us off on our way to Hebrew school after public school hours and beat us up. They were Protestants, I learned; so there just wasn't much difference between Catholics and Protestants. The Jewish kids organized to defend themselves. It was exhilarating. I was a leader of the Synagogue Youth Movement, however, and wanted to do more than just fight. I resolved then that I'd find the way to make peace, to be a bridge between the Jews and the Christians.

Interfaith Groups Begun

My father was then a leader in the Anti-Defamation League of B'nai B'rith and a supporter of the National Conference of Christians and Jews. He took me for the first time to a church for a brotherhood meeting. He spoke, and I was proud. The minister was the Reverend Daniel Poling, and I held the idea for quite a while that Baptists were different.

There was one funny incident about that meeting, however. The church song leader asked us what hymn we Jews would like to sing. I scanned the title list quickly and called out, "Rock of Ages," the title of our Hanukkah (Jewish festival) hymn. The Jews nodded assent; we all knew the title. How embarrassed I was when I realized that these words and tune were different, and christological at that!

It was not easy for us to say "Jesus Christ." In fact, I always skipped the words when we had to sing Christmas carols in school, although I felt that too was a result of an anger I had to overcome.

So I became the youth leader, the "front man" as it were,

when the adults of Philadelphia organized for the first time a human relations program and interfaith youth councils. This was due in part, I am sure, to the interreligious conflict in that city.

The minister in the neighborhood where the Nazi Bund had been organized, a German Lutheran, had a beautiful daughter, named Katherine. She and I became good friends. I desperately wanted to ask her to a party, but how could I? It would be wrong, first of all, to ask a "shiksa" (Christian girl), a German at that, and a minister's daughter no less! I used to dream that we married and put to shame the prejudice of the adults around us.

But I talked to Katherine quite a lot and received my first instructions in the beliefs of Christians from her. She helped me understand for the first time that Christianity could never countenance the pogroms that embittered my grandfather or encourage the Nazi attacks of the hoodlums. She encouraged my activities in the work of brotherhood.

More importantly in the long run, she challenged me to learn to recite *my* faith as she could hers. In religious school I had studied Hebrew, history, holidays, and celebrations, but I was never taught the why and the what of Jewish beliefs. She gave me the reason to know more. I asked my teachers hard questions, and my Jewish education benefited from my talks about Christianity.

Mrs. Strahan, Katherine, and Daniel Poling—all were my childhood symbols of the fact that a man can be decent to his fellow men even if he is a Christian. In truth, it is *because* he is a Christian that he can be.

There is another significant anecdote that had a bearing on my young life. I ran for freshman class president at college, and my opponent was George Belove, a fellow cheerleader and a sophisticated "High-Episcopalian type." Not all the students realized that I was Jewish—my name and looks were not—nor that I was even then bound for rabbinical school.

An anti-Semitic whisper campaign was started against me. It boomeranged; I defeated George by a larger vote than ever before in class politics. One classmate of mine, a girl from the Reformed Church in America, had transferred from her dorm room to another, because she rejected the anti-Semitism of her roommate. I loved Donna for that and asked her to the Victory Ball. When fellow Jews taunted me—a pre-rabbinical student dating a Christian—I was infuriated. Prejudice cut both ways.

The question of who was a Christian became a confusing one for me at one point in high school when I bumped into some "new-born" Christians. They scoffed at the other Christians I admired and offered to demonstrate their love for me by praying for my conversion. Behind their prayers was the threat that stiff-neckedness was rewarded by hell fire. I resented their haughty ways, their absolute assurance, and the arrogance of their prayers. I rejected their hell and their savior.

Interracial Work Revealing

It shocked me when I discovered that my father, although he was quite liberal in other ways, had a "thing" about Negroes. A first Negro family moved into the neighborhood. The very next day there was a junior high school dance. I danced with the new girl and came home proud and excited to share the news with the family. My father was livid. "Don't you ever dare dance with a Negro again," he warned. Others must have felt that way too. The girl transferred to another school within the week, and two months later the family moved out.

My father's injunctions only heightened the attractiveness

of Negroes for me, and so when I was in college I immediately joined an interracial youth club. The college sent me as its delegate to a youth assembly of the National Association for the Advancement of Colored People. Mine was one of three white faces in a sea of black ones. I was frightened; they talked differently and moved differently. I realized then what it meant to be a colored, racial minority and wondered how they must feel about me. White men had oppressed and harmed them. Now they were in strength and I was one of a minority, a white man in a black world. I couldn't blame them if they wanted to attack me and do me harm. Of course, that never happened.

There was a dance, and I wanted to ask one of the Negro girls to dance with me; but my father was still too big an obstacle. At the assembly meeting a speaker took off on Aunt Jemima and Little Black Sambo. I asked my neighbor innocently why Negroes were so perturbed. After all, I had learned to love that Negro aunt, the cereal was my favorite, and Little Black Sambo was a delightful child's book. He suggested that I express my sentiment publicly. I was wise enough not to.

Later I understood the Negro's anger at these condescending stereotypes that, even when favorable, denied Negroes their individuality and seemed designed to keep Negroes in "a place." It took me a while to overcome the guilt of disobedience to my father on the race question and then to discover that oversolicitousness on my part was as offensive to the Negroes as prejudice.

Stereotypes Enslaving

Stereotype dies hard. When I was 25 I joined the staff of an interracial, interreligious youth conference sponsored by

B'nai B'rith Youth organization and the Protestant Council of New York. The Negro delegates were dressed in the costume of their neighborhood—pegged pants, ducktail haircuts, black leather jackets. They were loud and coarse. I thought to myself that if I were to meet them on the street alone at night in Harlem I'd be afraid.

In the course of the three-day encampment, however, many of the Negro young people emerged as the real leaders. These boys and girls were committed Christians. They told our sheltered, middle-class Jewish youngsters hair-raising stories of delinquency and how they saved gangs from the filth of the streets. Their Christian faith had ennobled them, inspired them, given them the strength to rise above temptation and despair and to achieve hope.

On our way home, a Negro boy with whom I had become friendly sat next to me. Pointing to my collegiate, tweed sport jacket, he said, "Rabbi Gilbert, you sure don't look like no rabbi. Man, you look like a bopster." Here, all the time, I had thought of them as "juvenile delinquents," while they were saying, "Dig that crazy rabbi." Together we had learned a lesson. Difference frightens. Stereotype enslaves. We reach some degree of humanity only when we overcome the barriers between us and know each other as persons.

The apple did not fall far from the tree. I consider it a fulfillment of my parents' wishes to continue in the work of Jewish-Christian understanding, a task that is now my vocation. In fact, it was in fulfillment of their spirit, even if in correction of their error, that I also devoted myself professionally in later years to the work of racial justice. These childhood anecdotes, seen now from the vantage point of their consequences, strengthen me in my personal delight with my occupational choice. But it is not just the joy of work in the cause of justice. There is more to it than that.

I believe that God makes himself manifest to man through man. We are all created in God's image, and that spirit of God which is in each man speaks words more powerful to each heart than the spoken word itself. If we close our minds and eyes to the condition of another because of his race, religion, or ethnic background, then we deny God an opportunity to speak to us.

I feel my life has been enriched, because my heart was touched by a Lutheran minister's daughter, a Baptist preacher, and a rough-and-tumble Harlem boy. But it was God who spoke to me through them. My kindly teacher-God still has an assignment for me. It is "Love your neighbor as yourself"—and that is a lifetime job.

2

∽∽∽

A Short History of the Relations Between Jews and Christians

DURING THE DARK DAYS of 1938 when Nazi brutality threatened European Jewry and all of the world, Pope Pius XI interrupted his reading from a prayer book brought to him by Belgian pilgrims. A passage in the missal asked God to accept the prayers of the Catholics with the same delight with which He once accepted Abraham's willingness to sacrifice his son Isaac. The Pope declared: "Mark you, we call Abraham our father, our ancestor. Anti-Semitism is incompatible with the sublime thought and reality expressed in the text . . . Through Christ and in Christ we are of the spiritual lineage of Abraham. Spiritually we are Semites."

By that declaration the Pope not only affirmed the fact that anti-Semitism was a sin against God, but he was suggesting that Christians are one in spirit with Jews. Thus the Pope attacked the Nazi racist theory that Semites—the descendants of Noah's son Shem, from whom Jews derive—are an inferior race.

The Pope was also recalling that Christians were once all Jews. Jesus was Jewish as were his mother and father and his earliest followers. The teachings of Jesus draw upon and reflect his Jewish education. Christianity thinks of itself as sharing the promises God made to the people Israel through the patriarchs, Abraham, Isaac, Jacob, Moses and the prophets. The Jewish Bible is accepted as part of the Christian Bible. The psalms of the Jewish Bible are a major part of Christian prayer services. Many of the customs of Judaism are incorporated in Christian ritual.

One would expect that since Jews and Christians share such a beautiful tradition, they would have been close friends. Not so. Perhaps because they were so close, yet different, like members of one family, their quarrel with each other was severe and emotional. Of course, there were moments in history when Jews and Christians befriended each other and lived by the ideals of love and justice that are part of the Judaeo-Christian heritage, but for most of history we have quarreled, humiliated, and hated each other. Only in recent years have Jews and Christians rediscovered each other as human beings and begun to behave properly as brothers to one another.

When Christians Were Jews

The earliest Christians were all Jews. They observed Jewish holidays, made annual pilgrimages to the Temple in Jerusalem. They read and studied the Torah and the words of the prophets. They observed Jewish religious laws dealing with circumcision, Bar Mitzvah, the observance of the Sabbath, and the eating of kosher food. But there was one important difference: They believed that Jesus (in the Hebrew: Joshua or Jeshua), of Nazareth was the Messiah long promised by the prophets.

A Jewish Conception of the Messiah

According to traditional Jewish belief, God will appoint a redeemer *in a time-to-come*. Under the leadership of this Messiah (in the Hebrew: Moshiach, anointed one), the Hebrew people will be restored to national independence, the scattered in exile will return from their dispersion, men and nations will recognize that the God of Abraham is Lord over all the earth, and all men will live in tranquillity. God's law of justice will prevail. Some of the Jews also believe that at that time all the dead will be raised up to a restored life in order to stand judgment before God, and those whom God favors will spend eternity in the joy of God's Presence.

Such beliefs in an extraordinary change of circumstances once the Messiah appears provided Jews in that period with hope and courage, for their lives were otherwise quite grim. To understand this fact more fully, we must go back in time to an earlier period in Jewish history.

Jewish History before the Birth of Jesus

The Maccabean heroes of the Jewish rebellion against Greek-Syrian rule had established a dynasty that unfortunately became corrupt with success. Simon, brother to Judah Maccabee, was the ablest administrator of the Hasmonean dynasty. Under his rule as high priest the nation, Judah, was happy. It continued to prosper and grow also under the leadership of Simon's son, John Hyrcanus; but John had military ambitions. He conquered many nations and converted some of them forcibly to Judaism. When John Hyrcanus' son, Aristobulus, continued in that oriental despotic course, even slaying members of his own family who might be a threat to his power, the Jewish leaders under the influence of the Pharisee rabbis rebelled. They were concerned, also, lest the political power of the King and the religious power of the high priest, now identified in one person, permit pagan customs and values to break down the discipline of the Jewish faith. Bloody civil war plagued the Jewish State for a dozen years until at last the Jews lost their freedom with the conquest of Jerusalem by the Roman General Pompey in 63 B.C.

Then, for another quarter of a century, Judah suffered plunder and bloodshed. Harshest of the rulers supported by Rome was King Herod, whose ancestry can be traced back to an Idumean family forcibly converted to Judaism during the conquests of John Hyrcanus. When the Jews opposed Herod's rule, the Roman armies slaughtered them mercilessly and plundered the lands so devastatingly that even Herod complained: "Would the Romans deprive Jerusalem of all its inhabitants and possessions and leave me a king of the wilderness?"

At least 100,000 Jews were killed in that period of carnage and thousands were taken into slavery. To make matters worse, after the death of Herod there followed a devastating earthquake in 31 B.C., and seven years later crop failures brought famine, plague, and pestilence.

Herod's son, Archelaus, inaugurated his reign by murdering 3,000 people in the Temple court at the time of the Passover celebration. At last, in 6 A.D. Rome heeded the appeals of both Jews and Samaritans and banished the cruel king to Gaul.

Rome then abandoned the use of native rulers and instead placed Roman procurators over Palestine. Most of these attempted to Romanize the Hebrews, only further inflaming the Jews. They taxed the people grievously. The Jewish historian Josephus, describing these procurators, said, they are "like flies on a sore, but those already sated with blood do not suck as hard as the newcomers." Although the Sanhedrin, the supreme Jewish judicial body, was permitted to retain control over religious affairs, each year the procurator would sell the office of the high priest to the highest bidder. Then the Roman ruler manipulated the Jewish religious officials in order to serve his own purposes; thus the Sanhedrin remained effectively within the control of Roman rule.

One of the most insensitive of the Roman procurators was Pontius Pilate. During his administration Jesus was sentenced to death.

It is understandable that during such years of turbulence some Jews, such as the Essenes, would withdraw from the mainstream of political life and seek to live pious, God-fearing lives within their own communities. Most of them turned their back on violence of any sort. Others, such as the Pharisees, devoted to the religious practices of their faith, prayed desperately for the promised Messiah who would redeem the people from such oppression, and in the meantime they tried their best to maintain order, discipline, and hope within the Jewish community. The Zealots sought to hasten the day of independence by force of arms. Unfortunately also, some of the wealthy landowners and merchants, the Sadducees, found Roman rule much to their profit, and in league with the high priesthood they maintained an alliance with the Roman rulers.

The Roman procurators understood correctly that Jewish Messianic aspirations included a promise that the hated

Roman rule would be overthrown. This explains why Pontius Pilate, in cooperation with the corrupt Jewish priesthood and the Sadducees, viewed with alarm the claim made that Jesus was the Messiah or the King of the Jews.

The Ministry of Jesus

Jesus was born of Galilean parents about 4 B.C. (a mistaken calculation, later corrected by scholars, explains why the date of Jesus' birth was thought to have occurred four years earlier). Christian texts record that Jesus was deeply impressed by a zealous ascetic preacher called John the Baptist, whose style of living in the desert recalled that of the prophet Elijah. With stirring eloquence John called upon the people to repent of their sins. He warned them that the Kingdom of Heaven was near. The Hebrews flocked to John in large numbers. He baptized them in the River Jordan, a rite signifying their moral purification. The Hebrew prophets had foretold that Elijah would first appear and declare the coming of the Messiah. Jesus, therefore, was considered by his followers to be that redeemer and John the Baptist a manifestation of Elijah.

Jesus was a forceful and persuasive personality. The New Testament records many miracles of healing which he performed. His teachings were wise and compelling. He sought out with tenderness particularly those who were outcasts in Hebrew society. In those dark and troubled days hundreds of Jews gathered about him seeking inspiration and hope.

Believing that God's Kingdom was soon to appear, Jesus placed his emphasis on the religious ideals of Judaism, setting them above considerations of material well-being, political order, family responsibilities, and ritualistic requirements.

Thus he called on men to forsake their families if necessary, distribute all of their possessions to the poor, and prepare themselves for God's imminent salvation. Jesus called on his followers to love the enemy, return good for evil, forego violence, and to be pure in thought as well as deed. Although most of the teachings of Jesus are within the spirit of Judaism, he found himself in conflict with the Pharisees, the religious teachers of the Jews, particularly because he taught the law *on his own authority.* In Judaism no rabbi on his own has the power to make new religious law. A procedure existed by which the requirements of the faith were defined and enacted. To abandon the discipline of that procedure, especially during a chaotic period of history, was considered disastrous. But even more irritating to the Pharisees was the fact that Jesus seemed to imply, and his followers later asserted it as a matter of conviction, that Jesus was God. The Christian claim is that Jesus was God incarnate; that is, God having assumed human nature offered himself as a sacrifice in order to redeem men of their sinfulness. In the Christian concept of the Trinity, God is manifest in three persons, as Father, Son, and Holy Spirit. Such an identity of the Messiah with God is blasphemous according to Jewish tradition. Judaism holds that man and God are never one and the same.

Jesus was in trouble also with the Roman procurator and his vassal priests, and this brought about his ultimate undoing; for the rumor was prevalent that Jesus was the King of the Jews, a redeemer and a savior of the nation. Credence was lent to this claim when in an act of sensational boldness, upon entering Jerusalem at the time of Passover, Jesus drove the traders out of the Temple court and physically overturned the tables of the money changers. Passover had been the occasion before of rebellion against established authority. The pro-

curator took no chances. In league with the corrupt priesthood, he arranged for the death of this troublesome Jewish
leader and before the holiday was concluded Jesus was crucified *by the Romans.*

The death of Jesus caused a crisis among the followers of
the Nazarene, for in Jewish tradition the Messiah was to be
victorious, but obviously Rome was not overthrown nor did
the appearance of Jesus change the circumstances of the national life in any significant way. Some Jews remained convinced, however, that Jesus was the Christ. Their accounts
record that Jesus was resurrected and appeared to them on
the Sunday following his death. Trusting that he would soon
appear again, they maintained their lives as Jews, but kept
their own fellowship. In addition to the ceremony of baptism,
they continued the ritual of the Last Supper (the Passover
meal). They would meet for prayer and a meal that included
the Eucharist, that is, wine and a wafer of unleavened bread,
on the first day of the week, Sunday, the day of Jesus' resurrection.

The Separation of Church and Synagogue

It was chiefly through the organizational genius and missionary zeal of a convert to the faith of Jesus, Saul of Tarsus,
a freeborn Roman and a former Pharisee, that the Jewish
Nazarenes became a separatist church. Saul, the Paul of the
New Testament, once had been in the company of those Jews
who persecuted and harassed the Nazarene sect; but then, as a
result of a sudden overwhelming vision, Paul accepted Jesus
and devoted the rest of an active life to the spread of the
Gospel, that is, "the good tidings" that Jesus was the Messiah.

The Nazarenes had stimulated the wrath of the Jewish

leaders particularly because some accepted converts among the Hellenized Jews, gentiles, and Samaritans, without obliging them to obey Jewish religious law. One of these new converts, Stephen, was stoned to death, after he had provocatively preached blasphemous sermons within the synagogue and before the priestly Sadducean council. He was the first Christian martyr in the bloody history of Jewish-Christian conflict. Paul himself recounts that five times he received lashes from the Jews, three times he was beaten, and once stoned.

Paul was convinced that the disbelief of the Jews in Jesus was a sign that God intended to provide an occasion for the conversion of the gentiles. Paul did not seek converts, however, for a sect within Judaism; instead he offered a new religion based on belief in the crucified and resurrected Christ.

The New Testament records a bitter quarrel between Peter, leader of the Nazarenes in Jerusalem, and Paul over the requirements of Jewish law. A compromise was reached and the Jewish Nazarenes were allowed to observe Jewish practices, particularly circumcision and the dietary laws, whereas the gentiles were free of such obligations.

With the destruction of Jerusalem in 70 A.D. and the increased dispersion of the Jewish people, the gentiles in the new sect gained clear predominence. Paul elaborated a theology that justified their independence from the synagogue.

Paul taught that Jesus had fulfilled Jewish law. Men were required now only to believe in Jesus. In fact, Paul asserted that the Torah, the law, was incapable of assuring man's redemption from sinfulness and only faith in Jesus achieved the grace of God. God made a new covenant with mankind through Jesus, Paul asserted, adding that those who accepted the New Testament became the New Israel, the chosen people of God. Paul believed that at some future time the people from whom Jesus descended, that is, the Jewish people themselves, would accept Jesus as the Christ.

In order to counter the claim of the Jews that the crucified Jesus could not have been the Messiah, the gentile Christians reinterpreted the traditional Hebraic meaning of the mission of the Messiah to restore the nation. They emphasized instead the notion of rebirth, that is, they asserted that man was reborn through his faith in the Christ, and by that faith Christ would save men from the instincts and inclinations of the flesh that lead to sin. Furthermore, Christians were assured that just as Jesus had conquered death through the resurrection, so the believer would obtain immortality. Finally, in some future time, Jesus would reappear and Life Eternal would be given to those who have had faith in him.

Soon the Christians established a calendar of holidays based upon events in the life of Jesus: December 25, a date made official in the fourth century, commemorates his birth; New Year's Day his circumcision; Lent his temptation in the wilderness; Good Friday his crucifixion; and Easter his resurrection. The New Testament was added to Jewish scriptures in order to make up the Christian Bible. A church organization based upon patterns established and authorized by Jesus was instituted in the new church. It included a priesthood and bishops, and by the third century the Bishop of Rome had achieved predominence and was called Pope (from the Greek word *pappas* and the Latin *papa*, meaning father). The breach with the synagogue was complete.

Christianity Becomes an Official Religion

For the first centuries of its existence the church was only tolerated in the Roman world and frequently persecuted. The most ruthless effort to destroy the church took place in the reign of the Emperor Diocletian at the beginning of the fourth century. The faith of the Christians sustained them, however, and they inspired many converts. Then the Emperor Constantine, about 312, embraced the Christian faith and gave it a preferred position in the empire. In 380 Theodosius I named Christianity as the official religion of the Roman Empire.

During this period the leaders of the church met in various ecumenical councils in order to formulate basic doctrine and establish authoritative organizational patterns. The church claimed that it was the living body of Christ in the world and assigned to itself an authority quite in contrast to that of the synagogue, which is considered by Jews to be but one among many human agencies in the continuous effort of man to know God and to serve Him.

Armed with the support of the state, the church then engaged in a serious effort to unify all men within one faith, to root out heretics, and to curb other competing faiths. The Jewish religion was particularly suppressed, since the stiff-necked refusal of the Jews to accept a savior who had been one of them was particularly embarrassing. Furthermore, Jews insisted that only they were Israel and that the church had distorted the religion required of men by the God of Abraham. Finally, the Jews were themselves effective missionaries. The pious nature of their lives, their love of learning, their commitment to justice, the purity of their family devotion impressed the barbaric gentile world.

The earliest church regulations, therefore, were intended to diminish conversion to Judaism and to forbid Christians from engaging in any kind of social or business relationship with the Jews. At the very first ecumenical council the Emperor Constantine called upon Christians: "Henceforth let us have nothing in common with this odious people; . . . Our Savior has shown us another path."

Later church regulations and the teachings of a number of church fathers were intended to place Jews in a position of contempt. Basic Christian concepts were distorted as a conscious effort was made to inflame Christians and gentiles with an attitude of abhorrence toward the Jews. They were considered a people rejected by God, charged by the Christians as responsible for the crucifixion of the Christ. By their act of "deicide" (the killing of God), they had become accursed. They were to wander the face of the earth, homeless and friendless, a pariah people. Judaism was caricatured as a religion of legalism and hypocrisy.

Church-wide sanction to several degrading measures against the Jews were enacted by the twelfth Ecumenical Council held at the Lateran in 1215. These included an annual tax Jews were expected to pay the church and a requirement that Jews from the 12th year of age wear a badge distinguishing them from Christians. In Germany Jews had to wear a pointed hat, in Hungary a red cloth in the shape of a wheel, in England fringes of two colors, in Italy a yellow hat, in Spain Jewish males were prohibited from shaving their beards or cutting their hair.

In most Christian lands Jews were forced to live in restricted quarters, ghettos, denied permission to build or repair synagogues, forbidden to study the Talmud, made to attend sermons on Christianity, compelled to work in forced labor groups, and, most harmful of all, Jews were refused opportunity to own land or to obtain membership in a guild (required for work at a skilled craft), or to enroll at a university.

10,000 Jews were murdered in the Rhine Valley as the

Crusaders, on their way to drive out "the infidels" from the Holy Land, tested the edge of their swords on the Jews.

In 1492 the compulsory exile of the Jews from Spain ended a glorious history of Jewish achievement in that great nation. Thousands of *Marronos*—Jews who accepted the Christian faith and remained in Spain, but who practised their Judaism secretly—were burned at the stake by the Inquisition.

Fortunately, not all the princes of the church nor the lords of every land applied such harsh measures against all the Jews at the very same time, so that in one land or another Jews were able to find haven and protection. Several Popes issued decrees attempting to soften the harsh treatment of Jews and in particular to end the practice of enforced conversion; but nevertheless, for 1500 years the Jewish lot was a most unhappy one in Christian Europe.

The Protestant Reformation

"If I had been a Jew and seen such blockheads and locusts ruling and teaching Christianity, I would have become a swine rather than a Christian, because they have treated Jews like dogs and not like human beings." This is how Martin Luther, one of the great leaders of the Protestant Reformation, summed up his feelings about the Catholic persecution of the Jews.

The Protestants disagreed with Catholic teachings regarding the power of the papacy and the role of the priesthood; they also protested against abuses within church practice, such as the selling of dispensations. The Reformation succeeded particularly in those countries where the secular prince saw in the religious rebellion against Rome an opportunity to free himself from Roman political power.

Since Protestants asserted that spiritual authority was to be found not in the Pope, but rather in the Bible, and that each man was free in conscience to study and understand God's word, Martin Luther was sympathetic to the scholarly study of the Bible in the Hebrew. Luther's own Bible commentaries indicate that he was aware of Jewish teachings and commentaries. Luther hoped that the Jews would convert to the new form of Christianity he had helped to develop. When they did not, however, he was as vociferous in his denunciation of the Jews "and their lies" as he had been earlier in defending them from Catholic persecution. "I say to you lastly as countrymen, if the Jews refuse to be converted, we ought not suffer them or bear with them any longer." Thereafter, with but few exceptions, animosity and discrimination against the Jews continued as the general policy in Protestant as well as Catholic Europe.

The Emergence of Liberalism

With the arrival of the eighteenth century the last chapters of this dark, dank medieval period in European Jewish history were written. In that century there emerged liberal political voices who championed a new and novel idea. They suggested that differences in religion ought not be the basis for civil disabilities and that if all Jews were given freedom in economic and professional life and unrestricted educational opportunities all society would benefit. Such was the argument, for example, of Christian William Van Dohm, a Prussian counselor of state who authored a two-volume book entitled *Upon the Civil Amelioration of the Condition of the Jews*. In a like spirit the famous political philosopher, Montesquieu, satirically pointed to the persecution of the Jews as an example of barbarism still prevalent in so-called "Christian" Europe.

In the huge Austrian Empire under the rule of tolerant Joseph II, in France, Germany, and England liberal political leaders sought to enact legislation that would enable Jews to participate more fully in the political life or that would abrogate at least the most degrading of the restrictive and discriminatory civil disabilities. But, unfortunately, most Christian leaders continued to fear that such political reform would weaken the Christian character of the state. Thus they contributed religious arguments to the economic and political reasons given for denying full freedom to the Jews. The Archbishop of Canterbury in England, as late as 1834, opposed a bill that would have permitted Jews to sit in Parliament. His argument was expressed in these words: "The blessings of Divine Providence have been bestowed upon this country as a Christian country and the Archbishop should be apprehensive lest these blessings be withdrawn when the country cease to retain that character."

Only revolution of enormous proportion could overthrow this alliance of the clergy, the economically powerful, the politically conservative, and the prejudiced faithful who intended to keep the Jews in their place. The French Revolution, despite its bloody sordid excesses, accomplished that emancipation. In 1790 and 1791 the Jews of Napoleon's France were granted the right to citizenship; and in Italy, Germany, and Holland, even in Spain, wherever the French revolutionary forces carried their flag Jews were emancipated from the ghetto and placed on a new level of equality.

Not all of the enactments of Napoleon's regime were unalloyed blessings, however. For example, in 1806 Napoleon called together 112 of the leading Jews of France, Italy, and

Germany in order to obtain reassurances of loyalty to his regime and agreement to live by the civil law instead of their own religious law. Then, to administer his law as it related to the Jews, Napoleon established consistories in every French department which had more than 2,000 Jews. These consistories not only imposed restrictive regulations on Jewish religious life, but they tampered as well with Jewish economic opportunity. It was not until the separation of church and state in France in 1905 that the Jews finally won full freedom in that country.

It must also be remembered that the French Revolution represented a secular anti-clerical movement. The call was heard "to abolish Christianity and to establish a regime of Reason," and, in fact, even synagogues were burned and the observance of Jewish traditional rites made a "misdemeanor" under the law. Nevertheless, for the Jew the impressions made by these historic events were clear: liberals, who were non-religious or secular and who favored the removal of the church from its position of state influence, were leaders in the effort to emancipate the Jews, whereas the churches and clergy in general sought to maintain a Christian Europe and had denied Jews the fruits of freedom.

When Napoleon was defeated at Waterloo in 1815, reaction asserted itself and Jews were again subject to persecution and discrimination. In Italy, Pope Pius VII restricted Jews to the ghetto and permitted coercive missionary enterprises. In Spain, the Inquisition was renewed. Germany, fired by one of its greatest writers, Goethe, reimposed medieval disabilities upon the Jews. The Jews were expelled from Lubeck and Bremen, and from the faculty of the newly established University of Berlin. It was even suggested that Jews once again be compelled to wear a distinguishing "badge of honor."

But reaction could not keep liberalism long suppressed,

and everywhere Jews joined in liberal revolutions, winning for themselves, by their blood, an assured right to freedom and equality, if not fraternity. From 1830, when revolution restored liberty in France, until 1871, when the Papal States were wrested from church control in Italy, the Jews throughout Western Europe gained back the civil rights that had originally been promised them by the French Revolution.

From 1870 until World War I, and thereafter in Germany, anti-Semitism was the policy of growing reactionary political parties that sought to reverse the triumph of liberal democracy. In most countries the liberals, as part of their reforms, sought to curb church control over public education and end public support for church institutions. Thus it was possible to smear the democratic effort as a "Jewish conspiracy" and church leaders frequently joined in that defamation. The Jewish community on its part developed organizations that, to this day, not only seek to defend the rights of Jews, but also to marshal the resources of the Jewish community in defense of freedom for all men everywhere.

The right of Jews to civil liberties met its most severe test during the regime of Hitler in Nazi Germany, when the anti-Semitism latent throughout Europe was permitted to break forth in an officially sanctioned policy of murder. Unfortunately, the historic records indicate that in many countries in Europe, and particularly in Germany, anti-Semitism was given church support until, shocked by Hitler's excesses, church leaders realized that the harvest of hate was death.

The Situation in Eastern Europe

In Eastern Europe the situation was not very much different. Originally, fleeing persecution in Western Europe, Jews found safety for themselves in Poland and they considered it a promised land. But when in the early 18th century a change in economic fortune occurred in Poland, the Jews were the first to suffer. Although the Polish Catholic Church defended the right of the Jews to life, the clergy provided theological justification for anti-Semitic discrimination. In 1733 the Polish Church Synod explained: ". . . By their abject and miserable condition the Jews will serve as an example of the chastisements of God inflicted upon the infidels."

If life for the million and a half Jews in Poland then seemed difficult, it became worse when in 1772 the whole area came under the control of Czarist Russia. The reigning Russian Queen, Catherine II, charitably guaranteed the Jews their lives but she forbade them to join merchant and artisan guilds and confined them to certain *pales of settlement*.

In 1843 this policy of ghettoizing the Jews was made even more repressive through a series of edicts issued by Czar Nicholas I, a tyrant notoriously remembered in Jewish history as the Czar who introduced in Russia a 25-year program of enforced military conscription. This program was designed by the Czar to create Europe's outstanding army and to achieve as well the integration of Russia's many nationalities and religious minorities. Bearing down harder upon the Jews, however, Nicholas added six years to the 25-year period of conscription and drafted Jewish youngsters into the army at the age of 12. Then, employing the most cruel of coercive measures, he sought to convert these Jews to the Russian Orthodox Christian faith. It is estimated that in a 30-year period close to 100,000 of Russian Jewry's finest young men were compelled to enter the Christian church.

In 1881, under the rule of the Czar Alexander III, the Orthodox Church played an even more active role in the development of the nation's policy towards the Jews; and in the next several years the Jews suffered harsh pogroms, riots undoubtedly centrally organized to attack Jewish life and property. From that period until the climactic Easter pogroms in Kishinev in 1903 and the St. Bartholomew Day Massacre in the Odessa region in 1905, thousands of Jews were murdered, their property destroyed, and all with the blessings of church officials. The policy of the Czarist regime, as expressed by one of its ministers, was to solve the "Jewish problem" by the murder of one third of the Jews, the conversion of one third of the Jews, and the emigration of one third of the Jews.

Not only did the Jews suffer under the tyranny of the Czars, but so did all of Russia. Thus, when the Czarist regime collapsed before German attack during World War I, the land was fertile for the Communist Revolution. Unfortunately, one tyranny gave way to another. Hope never blossomed forth for the Jews in Eastern Europe and millions of Russian Jews achieved freedom only when they migrated to this country or to Israel.

The Situation of the Jews in America

The migration of Jews to the United States chronicles the history of Jewish oppression in Europe. The first Jewish settlers in America arrived in 1654. They were twenty-three Marronos, refugees from the Spanish Inquisition in Brazil.

A much larger immigration of about 200,000 German Jews arrived between 1815 and 1849. They were fleeing the re-emergence of Jew-hatred in Europe, a counter-reaction to the liberal reform which had been instituted during the Napoleonic era.

With the Pogroms of the early 1900's, two million more

Jewish immigrants sought the haven of these shores from Eastern Europe.

Finally, in recent years Jewish immigrants escaped to America from the brutalities of Nazi Germany and the totalitarianism of Communist Russia.

From the very beginning Jews found in this new land a greater measure of economic and social opportunity than they had ever experienced before. The frontiers were wide open and man was free to carve out his own destiny. But the securing of complete religious and political freedom in the United States had to be fought for. In pursuing that freedom, the Jews contributed to the development of democracy for all men in this country.

Although the American Constitution provided that "no religious test shall ever be required as a qualification to any public office or public trust under the United States," and although the First Amendment to the Constitution declared that "Congress shall make no law respecting an establishment of religion or prohibiting the free exercise thereof," these were only ideals that governed the policy of the Federal Government. They were not, at the very beginning, part of the practice of the states of the United States. The earliest settlers to the thirteen colonies brought with them European patterns of church-state establishment. The favored church or churches were supported by public funds, church morality and practice was enforced by the civil magistrate, and the members of minority religious groups were restricted in their freedom.

Thus, in North Carolina as late as 1808 an attempt was made to unseat a Jew who had been elected to the General Assembly. In Maryland it was not until 1828 that the electorate abrogated a constitutional requirement that one subscribe to the Christian faith in order to hold public office.

Christian leadership opposed President Abraham Lincoln's agreement to permit Jewish chaplains to minister to Jews serving the Union Army and there was a similar outcry in 1860 in the Christian press when a rabbi was permitted for the first time to offer invocation at the beginning of a session of Congress.

In most recent years the Supreme Court of the United States has ruled that prayers and devotional Bible readings may no longer be recited in the public school, a practice to which Jews have long objected. Studies indicate, however, that despite these rulings, there are hundreds of school districts in the United States that still conduct Christian Bible classes, nativity pageants, and revival meetings, and the Jewish minoriy in these school systems are given no consideration.

Anti-Semitism still exists in this country. Its ugly shape is to be seen in restrictions on opportunities Jews may exercise to live in an exclusive neighborhood or participate in a select social club or advance economically in certain industries. In its crudest form anti-Semitism is the most important part of the hate literature distributed wherever Negroes have engaged in any effort to achieve human dignity. As in Europe of old, any liberal effort to achieve freedom is branded a "Jewish conspiracy," and Jew-hatred is evoked by those who would maintain status quo patterns of discrimination.

New Trends in Jewish-Christian Relation

We have witnessed particularly since World War II in this country and in Europe a completely new and almost revolutionary trend in Jewish-Christian relations; just as the French Revolution brought with it political freedom for the Jew, so the scandal of Nazism and the consequent development of the State of Israel have overturned traditional Christian teachings concerning the Jews.

Meeting shortly after World War II in Amsterdam, Protestant leaders, through their World Council of Churches, confessed:

> We must acknowledge in all humility that too often we have failed to manifest Christian love toward our Jewish neighbors or even a resolute will for common social justice. We have failed to fight with all our strength the age-old disorder of man which anti-Semitism represents. The churches in the past have helped to foster an image of the Jews as the sole enemy of Christ which has contributed to anti-Semitism in the secular world. In many lands virulent anti-Semitism still threatens and in other lands the Jews are subjected to many indignities. We call upon all churches we represent to denounce anti-Semitism, no matter what its origin, as absolutely irreconcilable with the profession and practice of the Christian faith. Anti-Semitism is a sin against God and man.

At its third assembly in New Delhi in 1961, the World Council of Churches added to their statement this specific recommendation:

> The assembly urges its member churches to do all in their power to resist every form of anti-Semitism. In Christian teaching the historic events which lead to the crucifixion should not be so presented as to fasten upon the Jewish people of today responsibilities which be-

longed to a 'corpus humanity' and not to one race or community.

Recently, a Worldwide Lutheran meeting called to consider the relation of the church to the Jews, asserted:

Christian anti-Semitism is spiritual suicide. This phenomenon represents a unique question to the Christian church, especially in light of the long and terrible history of Christian culpability for anti-Semitism. No Christian can exempt himself from involvement in this guilt. As Lutherans we confess our own peculiar guilt and will admit with shame the responsibility which our church and her people bear for this sin. We can only ask God's pardon and that of the Jewish people.

Then the church called upon its constituency to examine their publications for possible anti-Semitic references and to remove and oppose false generalizations about Jews. "Especially reprehensible," says the report, "are the notions that Jews rather than all mankind are responsible for the death of Jesus the Christ and that God has for this reason rejected his elect-people. Such examination and reformation must also be directed to pastoral practice and preaching references." The Lutheran World Federation's Study Commission promised also "to oppose and work to prevent all national and international manifestations of anti-Semitism" and called upon its congregations and people "to know and to love their Jewish neighbors as themselves; to fight against discrimination or persecution of Jews in their communities; to make common cause with the Jewish people in matters of spiritual and social concern, especially in fostering human rights."

Similarly, Catholic scholars have begun to document how German bishops by their silence contributed to the Nazi murder of Jews. A past history of anti-Semitism coupled with an uncritical allegiance to the state stilled the prophetic voice of the church. Now the church, through an historic worldwide ecumenical council has officially reconsidered its teaching on the Jews, its attitude toward anti-Semitism, and as well the role of church and state in a pluralistic society. The late Pope John, seeking to give concrete expression to the church's new approach to the Jews, in an historic meeting with 130 leaders of the United Jewish Appeal, said to them, "I am Joseph, your brother." He also ordered the revision of Catholic liturgy that contained words and expressions offensive to the Jews.

Here in America both Catholic and Protestant educators have reviewed their religious school texts and are now rewriting them to assure a greater measure of understanding of Jews and Judaism. Any reference to Jewish suffering as a consequence of the crucifixion of Jesus is to be excised; for church teaching is that Christ was killed by the sinfulness in the hearts of all men and he is continually crucified when men harbor hatred against their brothers. Anti-Semitism is a sin against God and man, therefore, and cannot be countenanced by the church.

The churches have also come to recognize that they can no longer employ coercive measures to achieve the conversion of men. This violates the teaching of Christianity that God desires only that obedience which is freely given from the heart. Thus, church officials in recent years have issued decrees acknowledging the importance of religious freedom for all men and the right of man in good conscience to choose his own way in service of God.

Many Christians have also realized that the church is truly strong only when it receives its substantial support from its own membership. In countries where the church is still established and favored by the government, whether it be the Catholic Church in South America, or the Anglican Church in England, or the Lutheran Church in Sweden, attendance is poor and the church is weak. It receives its support through taxes and the people take the church for granted. Furthermore, where the church becomes thus dependent on the government, it finds it harder to criticize the state, as was the case in Germany. The church abandons its prophetic role. Thus Church officials in recent years have issued decrees acknowledging the importance of maintaining a distinction between the purposes and methods of the state and those of the church.

Finally, church leaders have come to realize that if they are to overcome the scandal of Christian disunity, they must stop quarreling with each other and begin listening to each other. The ecumenical movement which has emerged in recent years acknowledges that some measure of God's truth is nurtured and maintained within *other* churches, and that Christians are called upon to engage in dialogue with each other in order to appreciate that which God may be saying to all men through these religious differences.

This constructive attitude, now apparent in the relations between Protestants, Orthodox, and Catholics, is to be seen as operative also in the new relations between Jews and Christians. Christians are appreciating now, as they once did of old, that God had revealed Himself first to Abraham and then through His people elect, the children of Israel. Although the Jews suffered much in history, this was a suffering occasioned by their faithfulness to God and brought upon them cruelly by Christians and gentiles. Now, with the emergence of the State of Israel, Jews give evidence of a new dynamic purpose. Surely God must still be with this Hebrew people! Certainly He is still faithful to them! Thus church leaders have issued decrees calling for study and conversation with the Jews for the purpose of achieving mutual understanding and esteem. They wish to understand better that truth which is of the Jews.

This is not to assert that all is without difficulty in the relation between Jews and Christians, for there is still anti-Semitism to be found among some church leaders. There are many in the Christian church, in one country or another, who have not yet recognized the significance of the separation of church and state, nor the importance of religious freedom for all men, nor the vital contribution that Jews in their Judaism have to make to the religious vitality of our civilization.

Yet, so radical has been the change in attitude within world Christendom that Jews, on their part, have now become willing for the first time in history to engage in religious conversation with Christians without fear or anxiety. And as a result one can expect that Jews will attain to a deeper understanding of the meaning of the Christian faith for the Christian and a truer awareness of how much it is that Jews and Christians share together.

The likelihood, however, is that despite this new rapprochement, Jews and Christians will continue to remain in theological disagreement because of the basic Christian claim that Jesus is the Christ. As part of the Hebraic biblical tradition, Jews and Christians nevertheless share certain values and ideals together. These ought to influence our social outlook and our political judgments and lead us to cooperate together, wherever we can, to support efforts to achieve human freedom for all men, economic security for the needy, and the guaranty of peace. In working for such purposes, Jews and Christians will not only fulfill God's will upon earth, but rediscover each other as brothers.

3

~~~~~~

Anti-Semitism in the
United States

SHOCKED BY THE EVIDENCE everywhere around him of religious intolerance, Thomas Jefferson early in 1776 bitterly wrote:

> Why have Christians been distinguished above all people who have ever lived for persecutions? Is it because it is the genius of their religion? No. Its genius is the reverse. It is the refusing of toleration to those of different opinion which has produced all the bustles and wars on account of religion.

Jefferson at that moment was being quite critical. The truth is that Christianity has inspired men to glorious examples of sacrificial love for one another and for that purpose they have journeyed even to the darkest ends of the earth. It is also the truth that Christians have behaved scandalously toward each other and particularly toward the Jew, whose presence in Christian civilization remains a disturbing phenomenon. One can discover among Christians both those who hate their brother and those who have learned that the proper service of God requires the love of their neighbor.

In order to justify their hatred and to clothe themselves in sanctity, anti-Semites in the United States, like anti-Semites everywhere, have invoked particular aspects of the Jewish-Christian relationship—the role of Jews at Calvary, their decisive rejection of Jesus as the Christ, and Jewish insistence on maintaining a distinctive group identity. But a review of American history reveals also that anti-Semitism partakes of many of the same qualities that are present in any form of inter-group prejudice; in fact, it is helpful to realize that some of the same secular purposes and methods involved in the Catholic-Protestant conflict and then the Jewish-Christian antagonism are now also evident in the struggle between racial-segregationists and Negroes. Hatred, no matter against whom it is directed, must ultimately produce within the bigot the same irrationality, paranoiac belief that a conspiracy is at work, close-mindedness and readiness to use violence, that we have witnessed throughout all our history.

In assessing anti-Semitism in the United States, therefore, I wish to underscore two paradoxes: 1) There have been periods of American history when Jews were confronted by Christians both as enemy and as friend. 2) As a victim of prejudice, the Jew has suffered not only because he was a Jew, but also because he was a member of a weak minority group and, therefore, the object of political, economic, and psychological manipulation no different from that suffered by other minorities.

The answer to the problem of anti-Semitism requires, therefore, a more sophisticated religious commitment, sensitivity to the particular historic factors involved in Jewish-Christian relationship, and finally, an active participation in every effort to eradicate discrimination in American society by strengthening our democracy.

It is impossible in this brief review to provide a detailed account of Jew-hatred in the United States. The following illustrations indicate, however, that at last we have reached the point in American history where we can dare hope that discrimination will be brought to an end—if only there be the will!

The first settlement of Jews in the United States, as we have seen in the last chapter, consisted of refugees from the Spanish Inquisition in Brazil. Fleeing Catholic oppression, they landed in 1654 in Dutch Reformed New Amsterdam, only to find that Governor Peter Stuyvesant considered them to be members of a "deceitful race" who would "infest and trouble" his colony. The same Peter Stuyvesant had also clapped into jail Dutch Lutherans when they in their turn sought the right to hold worship. Eventually, Peter Stuyvesant was ordered by the Amsterdam Chamber of the West India Company to give the Jews their freedom. Unbelievingly he wrote to his superiors: "To give liberty to the Jews will be detrimental . . . giving them liberty, we cannot refuse the Lutherans and Papists."

Even after the adoption of the Bill of Rights, the state constitutions of many of the American states provided civil equality only for Protestants. Catholics and Jews were restricted in their privilege to vote or in their right to hold elective office, as in New Hampshire, New Jersey, Maryland, North Carolina, and South Carolina.

It was not until 1826 in Maryland, for example, that the Scotch Presbyterian legislator, Thomas Kennedy, after repeated efforts, was able to convince his colleagues to extend "to those persons professing the Jewish religion the same privileges that are enjoyed by Christians." If the Jews paved the way for Lutherans in New York, it was a Presbyterian in Maryland who opened the door to the Jews.

Despite such disabilities, anti-Semitism was of little significance in America, so few were the Jews and so vast our frontiers. The kind of man you were counted more than where you came from or how you worshiped God. Not so, however, with regard to Catholics, particularly the Irish and German Catholics who poured onto these shores in large numbers during the mid-1800's. Many Protestants feared Catholic power. They were also reluctant to permit the emergence of a genuine religious pluralism. Thus, they took alarm when Catholics, insisting on their rights as American citizens, petitioned that Catholic children be excused from Protestant public school devotional exercises and Bible lessons or, failing in that, requested that their schools be supported equally with public funds.

In 1834 the famous inventor, Samuel F. B. Morse, gave nationwide expression to a Protestant fear that the Jesuits were plotting to deliver America to the Pope. His book *Foreign Conspiracy against the Liberties of the United States* became model for all bigoted exposes and alleged conspiracies to destroy this land—charges to be leveled later in American history against the Knights of Columbus, Jewish Bankers, Jewish Bolsheviks; in this day one hears similar rumors of an alleged Zionist-Communist conspiracy to mongrelize the races, or poison water with fluoride or weaken the military.

Nativist Protestants rallied their forces within such organizations as the Native American Association and the Grand Council of the United States of America and political power was sought for this viewpoint through the American Party. As the "Know Nothing" constitution declared, their aim was "to resist the insidious policy of the Church of Rome and *other foreign influences* against the institutions of our country by placing in all offices . . . none but native-born Protestant citizens."

By 1854 the American Party was able to elect governors in nine states. They also claimed the allegiance of 62 members of the Senate and 104 of the 234 members of the House of Representatives. Patently, anti-Catholic, there were nonetheless specific links between such anti-Catholicism and a similar hatred of "other foreign influences"—which included the Jews. It is not surprising, therefore, to discover in the campaign literature of the presidential contest between the American Party's Democratic candidate, Millard Fillmore, and the Republican party's candidate John C. Fremont, charges that "Fremont was a Jew and had been educated in the Mosaic faith." Nativist support of the Democratic party in fact, among other reasons, accounts for the Jew's firm devotion to the Republican party, shaken decisively only with the candidacy of Franklin Delano Roosevelt.

In 1887 the American Protective Association specifically sought to curb the immigration of Catholics and to defend the public schools from subversion—namely, to maintain unchanged Protestant religious exercises within the public school. To further these purposes Protestant nativists had developed seventy weekly magazines and the American Protective Association had chapters in twenty-four states of the Union. This was also the period of Jewish migration from Central Europe. These Jewish migrants were the disillusioned refugees from the failures of the democratic uprising against reactionary government in Prussia, Austria, Hungary, and Italy. More than 200,000 Jews sought the haven of these shores. A vital, educated, and liberal migration, these Jews organized here a network of fraternal and charitable associations, benevolent societies, and the institutions of Reform Judaism. It is not insignificant that one of the earliest social action efforts of the (Reform) Central Conference of American Rabbis was designed to remove sectarian services and teachings from public education, thus, placing them in direct opposition to the program of the nativists.

Unfortunately for the Jews, the Populist Party's candidate for vice-president in 1896, polling one million votes, was a notorious anti-Semite, Thomas E. Watson. He was also a candidate for the presidency in 1904. This Georgia Baptist lawyer edited the most popular of the nativist magazines, assessing therefrom a private fortune of $250,000. By his successful sale of poisoned literature, he set an example for another technique in the bigots' quest for power. Later in history, a congressional committee was to report that anti-Semites were distinguished, through the sale of hate literature, by an ability to fleece their constituencies of vast sums of money. Unfortunately, hatred "pays off" in the United States and in recent years it has become big business.

It was Watson also who introduced notes of sexuality in his diatribes against the Jews—another conspicuous feature of hate literature. One need only recall the anti-Catholic exposés of Maria Monk or the response still to be attained by invoking the image of the Negro's alleged lust for white American women. The occasion was the unfortunate rape and murder of a 14-year old Southern girl charged against a Northern urbanized 29-year old Jew, Leo Frank. Watson lasciviously

wrote: "Leo Frank was a typical young Jewish man of business, who lives for pleasure and *runs after gentile girls*. Every
student of sociology knows that the black man's lust after the
white woman is not much *fiercer than the lust of the licentious
Jew for the gentile*." (Italics in original).

Not only Watson's paper, but many others as well, linked
the "Israelitic Americans" and "Romanist Americans" as the
"enemies" of "Christian America."

Particularly during the Civil War, Jews were made the
whipping boy both in the North and in the South; the short-
ages of supplies and produce felt by both sides were attributed
to the manipulations of "Jewish traders." This myth achieved
to such an influence, in fact, that on December 17, 1862,
General Grant ordered Jewish merchants "as a class" to be
expelled from the battle area. The *New York Times* called
this incident "one of the deepest sensations of the war." Of
course, Grant was soon to realize that Jews were not the only
speculators and, in fact, there were many Jews whose commercial dealings were honest and whose assistance—much of
it of a sacrificial nature—was required in the war effort.
Grant apologized profusely to the Jewish community, but he
provides an example of two more factors at work in any kind
of prejudice: the improper tendency based on experiences
with only a few to make a judgment on an entire people, and
the use of anti-Semitism or any form of hatred to serve economic or political ends. In this case, the beneficiaries of the
restrictive order against the Jews—perhaps the instigators of
that order—were gentile speculators and traders who rid
themselves of Jewish competition by a little anti-Semitism.

It was during the Civil War, also, that Congress enacted its
first and only edict of religious discrimination. On July 1861,
Congress established a chaplains corps for the Union Army,

the chaplains to be appointed from "regularly ordained ministers of some Christian denomination." As a result of this restrictive order, Michael Allen of Philadelphia, who had been serving "the Cameron's Dragoon," was compelled to resign. At the urging of Jewish leaders and with the support of some Christians, President Abraham Lincoln called for the amendment of the law. Congress acted quickly, but it is instructive to note that even as some applauded this action, there were many official Christian bodies who considered the appointment of a Jewish chaplain as a sure sign that America was abandoning its Christian commitment. Those who abhorred this action also recalled the "infamy" of the Jews at Calvary.

If there were some Protestants who defaced the image of Christ by their hatred, there were others in this same period who recognized His image in the plight of their Jewish brother. Protestant clergymen in 1840, for example, rallied to a demonstration in Philadelphia condemning the blood-libel charge that had been brought against the Jews in Damascus. Franciscan monks, supported by the French Consul there, had charged the Jews with the murder of their superior, allegedly for the purpose of using his blood in the Passover rites. For eight months the Jewish community of Damascus suffered murder and pillage. Moved by Christian representations, President Martin Van Buren in one of the earliest actions of the Federal Government in behalf of an oppressed minority, extended "the active sympathy and generous interposition of the Government of the United States." Van Buren noted that among the Jews "are found some of the most worthy and patriotic of our citizens."

Again in 1858, Protestants joined with the Jews in seeking governmental intervention in behalf of the Moratora family, whose six-year-old son Edgar had been stolen away from his parents in Bologna and placed in a convent. Evidently Edgar had been secretly baptized by his Catholic nurse when severely ill and although the baptism had been administered without his parents' consent, the Holy Office of the Inquisition ruled that he must be raised as a Catholic. He was never again to see his parents.

Early in 1881, a series of pogroms erupted in Eastern Europe. As we have already seen, Alexander III had adopted as his policy for dealing with the Jewish problem the proposals of the Procurator of the Holy Synod of the Greek Orthodox Church, Constantin Pobyedonostzev: to force one third of the Jews to migrate, to baptize one third, and to starve the remaining third to death. On February 1, 1882, 100 prominent Christian leaders in New York, led by ex-President Grant, called for American action. Although this country could do little to stop the persecution of Jews—for some years we actually delayed the ratification of a treaty with Russia on this account—America could welcome to its shores Jewish families.

The period between 1881–1914 was a time of mass migration and industrial expansion and 22,000,000 migrants of every religious persuasion, chiefly from Eastern and Southern Europe, rushed through "the Golden Door."

Emma Lazarus, a German Jewish poet, was so moved by America's hospitality, that in 1883 she composed her sonnet "The New Colossus," whose immortal words were later to be inscribed on the Statue of Liberty. She sang:

> . . . Give me your tired, your poor,
> Your huddled masses yearning to breathe free,
> The wretched refuse of your teaming shore,
> Send these, the homeless, tempest-tossed, to me.

2,000,000 Jews accepted this invitation and, indeed, for them America was a golden land. No other ethnic or religious group can boast the same rapid climb-up the ladder of cultural, economic, and social success. It was exactly this rapid advancement of the Jew, however, that provided the occasion for a new form of social discrimination in the United States. As the historian, John Higham, points out: "Anti-Semitic discriminations offered another means of stabilizing the social ladder . . . The evidence suggests that insecure social climbers, rather than relatively more secure Patricians, first resorted to this means of reducing competition."

Thus, once again, the paradox. Even as America gave with one hand, there were some who would take away with the other.

Anti-Semitic agitators, Protestant nativists, the socially insecure, and even fearful liberals in the Labor Movement joined forces to close the door to immigration. In 1924 Congress adopted a shameful racist immigration bill.

From the World War I period on until the adoption of the Johnson Immigration Measure, America had witnessed a continual harangue of anti-foreign, anti-Semitic, anti-Catholic, and anti-Negro hatred. The address of Imperial Wizard Evans, before 75,000 Klansmen in Dallas, Texas, October 24, 1923, is representative: "Negroes, Catholics, and Jews," Evans asserted, "are the undesirable elements in America, defying every fundamental requirement of assimilation. They are incapable of attaining the Anglo-Saxon level." Jews were specifically accused of being an "absolutely unblendable element" for whom "patriotism as the Anglo-Saxon feels it, is impossible."

Henry Ford's *Dearborn Independent*, a weekly newspaper with a circulation of 700,000 added another ingredient to the stench of hatred. Jews, Ford claimed, are engaged in an international conspiracy to rule the world. "Not only does the Jewish question touch those matters that are common knowledge, such as financial and commercial control, usurpation of political power, monopoly of necessities, and autocratic direction of the very news that the American people read; but it reaches into the cultural region and so touches the heart of American life." Ford's publication of *The Protocols of Zion*, an exposé of an alleged international Jewish conspiracy, has now become a classic in the literature of the anti-Semite. Ford himself repudiated the forgery, but Jews never really believed him, particularly when he later accepted Hitler's Grand Order of the Great Eagle of Germany on the occasion of his 75th birthday.

Inevitably the participation of some Jews in the Bolshevik revolution and then the depression of 1929, provided anti-Semites with all the evidence that they needed to step up their claim that "Jewish bankers" or "Jewish Communists" were involved in a worldwide financial manipulation or revolution, the exact charge depending, of course, on the bigot and the gullibility of his audience. Even the halls of Congress echoed with such charges. So widespread were these canards, that the editors of *Fortune* in February 1936 devoted an entire issue to the role of Jews in American finance. Almost with disbelief, considering the currency of these rumors, *Fortune* exclaimed: "Indeed, there are practically no Jewish employees of any kind in the largest commercial banks and this in spite of the fact that many of the customers are Jews." *Fortune* also revealed that the largest Jewish investment house in America, Kuhn & Loeb, held only 2.8% of the foreign loans outstanding among American investment banks. We see here another model of the hatemongers' technique—the exaggeration of the power and influence of the object of his hatred.

Hitler's rise to power in Germany had its serious repercussions in the United States. As the House un-American Affairs Committee has revealed, hundreds of anti-Jewish organizations bounded into existence. The Committee listed 135 of them. They were not insignificant. Fritz Kuhn's "German-American Bund" claimed a membership of 25,000. Its Madison Square rally was attended by 19,000 and from the rafters a sign shouted: "Wake Up America. Smash Jewish Communism. Stop Jewish Domination of Christian America."

William Dudley Pelley's "Silver Shirts" reported to the Internal Revenue a $50,000 a year financial turnover. He distributed one million pieces of anti-Semitic literature each year.

Father E. Coughlin spewed forth anti-Semitic diatribes every week to a radio audience of three million. His charge that the Jews were aligned with the Communists, stimulated a latent anti-Semitism to be found among Catholic Americans and planted the seeds of a suspicion that remains among some Catholics to this day.

No wonder, then, that the Jewish community expanded the work of defense agencies such as the Anti-Defamation League, the American-Jewish Committee, and the American-Jewish Congress.

With the end of World War II, however, America entered a new era. The Jews had demonstrated their allegiance with their blood. Americans realized the bitter price civilization must pay for hatred allowed to run rampant. Without question, a resolve was evident nationwide that once and for all discrimination should be buried in this land.

The national effort to end racial segregation is evidence of this resolve in action. Yet again, hatemongers and right wing extremists are at work. Some of these are the same Nazis and anti-Semites who were in operation prior to World War II. Their newspapers cry out the alarm that the Civil Rights Movement is allegedly under the domination of Zionist-Communists. The National Council of Churches, it is claimed, has sold out to the Jews, and America itself is in danger of subversion from within.

I have no doubt that good Americans will repudiate decisively the National States Rights Party, the revived Ku Klux Klan, the John Birch Society, and any other extremist group that will rear its head.

Jewish community relations agencies reveal that anti-Semitism is now at its lowest point, particularly in those areas where they have devoted their major educational energies. In the most recent 20-year period, restrictive quotas on admission of Jews in professional schools has almost been eliminated and resort hotel discrimination is virtually extinct. Unlike a former period, the use of anti-Semitism in a political campaign today is sure to doom the candidate to failure.

Yet recent surveys reveal, also, that 72% of private clubs and 60% of city clubs still discriminate on grounds of religion. Jews are still barred from upper eschelon positions in banking, insurance, and in the best law firms. They are still denied housing in the most exclusive communities. 32% of Americans in 1960 confessed that they were uncertain or would not vote for a president nominated by their own political party if he were a Jew, even if he were well qualified. Jews cannot forget so easily that just five years ago, in 1960, during the German swastika epidemic, there were also 700 incidents of anti-Jewish desecration reported in the United States over an eight-week period.

It appears to me that the time is now for Americans to end such nonsense. "What ye do to the least of these, ye do to me."

It is also well here to recall H. A. Overstreet's warning that the main problem stems not from those who impose restrictions against Jews, but from those who acquiesce to them. Said Overstreet:

He who permits evil, commits evil. This is what makes for the haunting sense of guilt in our culture. Many a member of the dominant group will earnestly aver that *he* never intended that Negroes should be insulted and maltreated . . . that *his heart* is sore and ashamed when he reads of the defiling of Jewish synagogues by hoodlums. He did not intend these things, but *he created the social sanction for these things.* By adopting a twisted principle of human association, he and the people like him open the Pandora's box out of which have flown the intolerance and cruelties that have defiled our culture.

4

Reform Judaism in the United States 1890–1965

How has the American experience shaped Reform Judaism; and in what ways, in return, have the rabbinical leaders of Reform Judaism through their Central Conference of American Rabbis contributed to this country? The answers to such questions are not easy to come by, most importantly because social scientists themselves find it hard to define those values or those attitudes towards life that characterize America. As Professor Robin M. Williams, Jr. has warned: "Any attempt to delineate a national character or typical American values . . . is extremely hazardous."

ON DEFINING THE AMERICAN SCENE

Such an effort to define the American character, and to describe the sources in American history that account for its development was inaugurated several years ago by the Center for the Study of Democratic Institutions. Sixty leaders of thought, representatives of management and labor, religion and the arts, social engineers, political scientists, civil rights leaders, psychoanalysts, economists, historians, and editors convened in Washington, D.C. for five days of conversation. The result was chaos. It was evident, after all, that each of us understood America differently. We had read American history from different texts. Our hopes and dreams for America reflected more on the inner quality of our individual value commitments than on the concrete measurable, external factors of the American scene. Perhaps the trouble was that we were overly educated, self-generating, particularly articulate persons. There may have been a different result had just plain grass-root Americans spoken their minds. There may have been a different result, also, had we been matched with an equivalent number of leaders from Europe, Africa, or Asia; then we might have discovered our particularity as Americans. It seems obvious however, that no one can simply postulate what is uniquely "American" about our character, viewpoints, or values.

For example, American Catholic prelates at the Vatican Council acted as though the statement on religious liberty was a matter of particular American interest and a contribution of the American historic experience to the theology of the Church. The truth is that the statement's most articulate, persuasive, and radical theoreticians came from Europe and Africa, for they too are experiencing the painful challenge of pluralism, and having reflected upon its significance with such an intensity, they joined their strength to a broadly based consensus. From the worldwide perspective the American experience of religious pluralism is no longer unique.

In the paradox of history, also, the very content of words can assume radically opposite meanings and each new advance brings with it new opportunity and new problems. The fast flow of history makes it impossible at any point to separate out all the elements and then reconstruct them again. Rabbi Eugene Lipman at that Washingon meeting, for example, sagely observed that when we talk about pluralism in America's society today, it is not the pluralism of the nineteenth century. "The first immigrants," he observed, "were revolutionaries over against the society from which they ran away, but the volatility, individualism, and excitement of the ethnic, religious, and racial groups that came to this country soon began to disintegrate . . . Every time Americans stayed in one place long enough to get together and become a stable community, they began to homogenize." Then Rabbi Lipman added: "We Jews are probably freer today to express ourselves than we ever were, but we don't want to express as much Jewishness as our grandparents did a hundred years ago . . . Something bland seems to come into our characters when we have been Americans long enough."

To bring the paradox up-to-date, I would add the observation that new confidence in the democratic process has stimulated each of America's religious groups to play a more vigorous role in the shaping of American society and the result has been an increase in controversy today over such old issues as prayer in the schools, public funds for the church-related schools, Sunday closing laws, and so forth. Thus, with all the blandness a sharp new awareness of our individuality and separateness has again emerged in modern day America.

At one point in history the "liberal," frequently a protestor against the alliance of Catholic clerical power and the feudal state, insisted on the right of the individual to freedom of conscience. This regard for the dignity of the individual gave root to democracy and the development of laissez-faire capitalism. Yet at another point in history, that liberalism unchanged has become the most extreme form of conservatism, for the economic problems encountered in capitalism require collective action, social planning, and state intervention. The fundamentalist Protestant, once a flaming liberal, now finds that loyal adherence to his traditional value commitments brands him as a "reactionary."

If Americans pride themselves on their commitment to individuality and the freedom to individual choice, we are today confronted by the fact that many have used that freedom to achieve the most rigid forms of cultural and social conformity.

If Americans pride themselves that we have achieved a democratic system than enables social change to take place in a peaceful, evolutionary pattern—or so it appears in contrast to Asia or South America—we are also confronted with the harsh reality that riots, harassment, intimidation, cross burnings, boycotts have also accompanied every decisive change in the status quo arrangements between America's religious and racial groups. Furthermore, commitment to peaceful democratic evolution, demanding order and proper procedure, has hidden from our view the possibility of radical alternatives in political and economic organization. Our Republican and Democratic Parties are rarely the custodians of significant differences in outlook or opinion.

At the Washington conference Justice William O. Douglas asserted: "America's strength is not in fire power, but in ideas of justice, tolerance, equality. We have a decisive role to play; and we have on our side assets which will make it easy for us to win the contest. We have the Declaration of Independence,

Abraham Lincoln, and the Bill of Rights . . ." But Michael Harrington countered: "Power, not ideas, define America for the rest of the world . . . We are personified by our oil companies, sugar companies, and the like. We are the status quo in the world . . ."

In similar vein Max Lerner in his classic work *America as a Civilization* has noted that our country's main stream religious orientation includes vestiges of "17th-century Calvinism, 18th-century deism, 19th-century rationalism, and mid-20th-century anxiety. No wonder," he writes, "there are contradictions in the relations between God and man." Lerner points out "America is as secular as a culture can be where religion has been intertwined with the founding and meaning of society. It is also as religious as a culture can be whose life goals are worldly and whose daily striving revolve not around God, but around man." The Supreme Court protects atheism and there is a deep strain of religious nonconformity in the American heritage, yet there is also less and less room for the godless in America where "godlessness" is associated with communism and depravity. Lerner concludes:

> Every generalization about American thought can be offset by a counter-generalization . . . If you note how much of American thought has been secular and rationalist, you are confronted in reply by the tradition damning the merely rational . . . If you deny tragic depth in American thought, there are Hawthorne and Mellville to refute you. If you say that American thought has been a feet-on-the-ground realism, you must correct the picture with the millenialist tracts formed by the experimental communist settlements . . . Finally, if you say that American thought—like the American class system

—remains pluralistic . . . and was hostile to any scheme of rigid determinism, a minority report would note the determinism of Frederick Jackson Turner, of Henry and Brooks Adams, of Veblen and Beard . . . Always there has been the steady beat of change in American life.

The participants at that historic Washington consultation not only disagreed on any definition of the American character, they also differed on which institution shaped that character. Value formation was seen as turning upon business and technology. Observed Perry Miller, "Actually America is a business civilization." Added Eric Larabee: "The seeds of Democracy are inherent in mass production . . . What is bad for the machine is also bad for the men who work for them." A cure for all the faults of American character was seen to reside in the development of good government. Said Irving Kristol: "The basic things I object to today, even those things which seem to reside in our character, are essentially political." Whereupon Rabbi Robert Gordis, testifying to the role of religion in shaping American character, argued: "A divorcement between politics and ethics is by no means inevitable if we adopt . . . the necessary framework for ethics. We need a wider exploration of the sources of natural law . . . than we now possess . . . The historical fact remains that religion has supplied much of the dynamic for protest against social evil . . ." And Will Sparks, unconvinced, muttered: "The need for religion, the goodness of religion in human life, is something that remains to be proved. It has not been demonstrated to my satisfaction that more good than evil has been done in history in the name of God."

Oscar Handlin has said: "Once I thought to write a history

of the immigrants in America. Then I discovered that the immigrants *were* American history."

We propose in this chapter, therefore, no definitive analysis of the American impact on Reform Judaism, nor do we know how to measure Reform Judaism's contribution to American culture. But of this we are certain: Our experiences are part of American history. What we are and what has happened to us and how we have responded in turn, is as much an ingredient of American life as that of any other immigrant group, and all Americans are immigrants. At best we can only underscore some of the normative or main motifs in the relation of American Reform Judaism to American society, aware at all times that in reaction there are counter-tendencies, other viewpoints, differing experiences, for just as America remains hard to define, so is Reform Judaism; its liberalism, its openness to fresh points of view have caused us to experience also "the steady beat of change."

CONTINUITY AND DISCONTINUITY WITH EUROPE

Reform Judiasm in Europe

Reform Judaism begins in Europe. It was set in motion by at least two impulses: one inner and the other external. The discipline and regimen of Halachik Jewish life had lost its emotional grip on many Jews. The law was observed, but with no feeling nor understanding of its deeply spiritual message. Much of the tradition had served defensively to bind the Jew together in a hostile world, to protect him in his uniqueness, and to perpetuate his dream of ultimate redemption in Zion. But paradoxically, its oppressive hold on the Jew also reinforced his alienation from the world. Screening out any new thought or philosophy, Jewish life sank deeper into self-impoverishment. The Napoleonic revolution, therefore, not only offered hope that the political, economic, and social restrictions imposed by a Christian dominated authoritarianism over the Jew would be ended, but it also enabled some Jews to break through the confines of rabbinism.

Napoleon smashed the ghetto and offered the Jews civil equality, but he also insisted that the Jew declare himself a Frenchman "of the Mosaic religion." By order of a Napoleonic instituted Sanhedrin of Jewish leaders, Jews bought their political freedom at the price of their community system, conceptions of nationhood, and the age-old religious dream of a restored Zion. French law was given authority over Jewish religious law and the Jews entered European society no more than a faith community just like the Christians. They no longer constituted a people, a state within a state. Their individualism was affirmed and their Judaism took on an ecclesiastical rather than a national dimension.

The French Revolution included secular anti-clerical impulses, which turned at times into an anti-religious fervor. As we have seen in Chapter 2, even synagogues were burned and the observance of Jewish traditional rites was a "misdemeanor" under the law. Nevertheless, to repeat, for the Jew the impression made by these historic events was clear and it still influences Jewish behavior: liberals who were nonreligious or secular and who favored the removal of the church from its position of state influence were champions in the effort to emancipate the Jews, whereas the churches and clergy in general sought to maintain a Christian Europe and, supported by authoritarian political power they denied the Jews the fruits of freedom.

Under such conditions the hope for political freedom stimulated reform in religion in at least these ways:

1. Through the weakening of the ecclessiastical authority of the rabbinate and rabbinical law and the emergence of laity as distinguished religious communal leaders;

2. Through the acknowledgment of primary loyalty to the political state as contrasted to the dream of a resurgent Jewish nationalism and the return to Palestine;

3. Through the acceptance of cultural and aesthetic forms that would promote integration into society and the abandonment of the ghetto;

4. Through the revision of synagogue practices and theological teachings to conform to new cultural standards and reflect scientific knowledge and the primacy of reason over mysticism.

After Napoleon's final defeat in 1815, Jews were again subject to persecution and discrimination. Liberal religion was assumed to harbor the seeds of liberal politics; and sad to say Orthodox rabbis, despite the mistrust they properly felt towards authoritarian government, made use of that reactionary governmental authority to repress the liberal experiments of the Jewish laity, particularly in Germany.

Thus Israel Jacobson's experiment in new liturgy was first halted by King Jerome, and then in Berlin by Frederick William III. As the historian Graetz explains: "The King of Prussia . . . was adverse to all innovations, even in Jewish circles, and hated them as being revolutionary plots." In such a soil a movement that depended upon freedom of conscience could not emerge. Liberal Jews had to seek elsewhere a more fertile soil for the development of Reform Judaism. They found it in America.

The Situation of the Jews in America Prior to 1848

Not more than fifteen thousand Jews were to be found in the United States by 1848. Jews migrated to these shores only in small numbers. They were swallowed up by the much larger Protestant population and scattered all over the colonies. On the eve of the American Revolution there were only three thousand Jews in a population of more than three million. Even so Jews made their mark. John Wesley, the noted Methodist leader, testified to the ethical quality of the life of America's pioneer Jews when he wrote of them in 1737 after his sojourn in Georgia: "I began learning Spanish in order to converse with my Jewish parishioners, some of whom seemed nearer the mind that was in Christ than many of those who call him Lord."

Although in Europe Sephardic and Ashkenazic Jews had only feelings of scorn for each other, in America they mingled freely with each other, discarding Old World patterns of class consciousness and ethnic pride. In America they were judged as individuals, given their freedom as individuals, and expected to contribute to their country as did all other citizens. The Jews were offered little occasion to maintain defensive patterns of group cohesiveness. Whatever religious life they sustained was maintained around their synagogues. It was voluntary and it reflected their freewilled choice.

The Situation of Protestants in America

In the mid-1800's the predominant Protestant community in America was in the midst of a religious awakening. The disestablishment of churches from state support after the adoption of the Constitution resulted in the decisive weakening of the Anglican and Congregational establishments. Now that church membership was no longer coerced, the number of enrolled Christians dropped considerably. It is estimated that at that period not more than 15% of the American people were members of any church. The frontier evangelist, the Methodist itinerant preacher, and the Baptist revivalist were the "free church" response to this crisis.

The most distinctive feature of this new awakening was individuality. More important than "Gospel discipline" was heartfelt consent. The transient evangelist, often self-ordained and as unlettered as his audience, offered individualistic interpretations of salvation. As the church historian, Edwin Scott Gaustad, has observed:

> Novelty was no sin. Tradition was a burden and improvisation was the rule and doctrine in polity and in morality—not to mention architecture and hymnology. Logically the ultimate improvisation was the creation of new denominations. Related to the acceptance of an indulgence in novelty was the loss of authority . . . Recognizing no ecclesiastical creed or political authority, the frontier churchman proudly asserted, even flaunted, the liberty which was for him a daily experience.

What authority existed was to be found in man's sincere effort to understand Scripture. "The New Testament could speak to every man, however encrusted by ignorance or sin, without the media of clergy, creed, or even church."

Alexander Campbell, in 1827, founded a new Disciples of Christ Church that attempted to gather under one banner "pious men of all denominations" whatever their creed and confession, so long as they were united by "a sanctifying baptism of grace," but in less than one half century this unifying eclectic effort itself became a denomination of more than 500,000 members.

In 1830, 24-year-old Joseph Smith called together five friends and from that beginning in Fayette, New York, the Mormon Church developed. Smith, confused by the claims of conflicting denominational appeals, decided that such strife was too great "for a person as young as I was to come to any certain conclusion who was right and who was wrong." Developing his own theology, Smith inspired his followers to join him in his westward trek. By 1870 there were approximately 200,000 Mormons.

Other American denominations that developed during this period included the Seventh Day Adventists and the Jehovah Witnesses, both of whom promised that Christ's appearance on earth was imminent. Holiness and Pentecostal churches also emerged, emphasizing the additional power of holiness, purity in life, and glossolalia that comes to those Christians who have received God's spirit in "all its fullness."

Such anarchy, however, was not long to be tolerated and most denominations attempted to make some order out of the chaos by building Bible colleges and seminaries. By 1850 there were 231 Christian colleges in the United States. They also developed congregational and ministerial associations that sought by the authority of their collective action to offer some direction to church development.

Both the pull to individualism and a remedial concern for church discipline through the theological school and the congregational and ministerial association are also reflected in the early experiences of Reform Judaism in America.

The Immigration of German Jews to America

Between 1825 to 1865, 200,000 disillusioned German-speaking Jews from Germany, Austria, and Hungary came to America. There had been no peace for them in Europe. The liberal revolution had failed. These German Jews had made an effort to become part of European civilization. They were among the more educated middle class. They were politically sophisticated. Some of them had experimented with religious reform in Germany and they knew about the opportunity they were to find in America. The widely respected German Jewish poet, Ludwig Kompert, called out to them: "(In America) A man is worth what he is and he is what he does. Before all else, be free—and go to America."

German Jews became part of a mass immigration wave from Europe to America, and by their immigration, therefore, they were not unique. They became America. Between 1841 to 1855, 1,600,000 Irish had arrived in America, half of them settling in New York, Pennsylvania, and Massachusetts. Next came 1,301,000 Germans, among whom were the German Jews, and these Germans traveled into the Midwest, Jewish peddlars and traders leading the way. As the American Jewish educator, Jacob Hartstein, has pointed out,

German Jewish peddlars were the first settlers in San Francisco before the gold rush. They settled in Oklahoma territory, in Texas, Oregon, Washington—in the Midwest, the South, the Southwest, and the Far West. The peddling frontiersmen brought needed commodities to the far-flung western settlers. They also brought news of the outside and acted as mail carriers . . . They carried vital medicines and some of them served as emergency physicians. They brought books and clothing, food and animal supplies and farm equipment and they made emergency loans . . . Without them the frontier settler could hardly have survived. They helped to open new markets and spurred increased production. Credit for the opening of the West is shared by the German Jewish peddlar with the actual homesteader. Both gave their best energies and their tireless labor so that new communities might survive.

America was congenial to all that Reform Jews brought with them from Europe: individualism in theology, experimentalism in liturgy, anti-clericalism, and denominationalism. These American religious characteristics allowed Reform Judaism to take root and flourish. America nurtured this unique expression of Judaism and in turn Reform Jews reinforced the voluntaristic nonecclesiastical character of American religiosity.

At first the German Reform Jews who had been proud of their Germanic culture, maintained themselves—as did other Germans—as Germans. Prayer and education was in the German language. The first Jewish prayer books were translations of a liturgy that had been developed in Germany.

As they were welcomed into America, however, Jews discovered that there was an opportunity here to achieve genuine brotherhood with the Christian in a fashion never before experienced. Thus the tendency to repress those practices and beliefs that were nationalistic in character or particularistic was reinforced. "We intend to hold communion with our God as a God of humanity," said one rabbi, "and not the God of a specially chosen race or people."

In a period described by American Reform Judaism's his-

torian, Beryl Harold Levy, as "fecund in prayer book manu-
facture," each rabbi or congregation created its own tradition.
Isaac Mayer Wise, father of American Reform Judaism, reflecting the new challenge of America, entitled his own effort
"Minhag America" (literally, according to the tradition of
America). Not until early 1900 were the Reform Jews able to
achieve agreement on one prayer text that would win the
acceptance of most Reform congregations.

Isaac Mayer Wise also attempted to fashion a theology that
would be rational, universal, and rooted in biblical sources.
He wrote in one of his essays: "The author of this little vol-
ume . . . reads the Bible from his own standpoint and proves
that it contains the complete and rational system of religion
for all generations and countries, a universal religion in perfect harmony with the Bible science and philosophy."

Reform leaders in America emphasized, as did their German predecessors, that Israel's mission was "to bring the
knowledge of the one and only God to all the children of
men." Some of the laws and rituals and ceremonies of rabbinic Judaism, they conceded, testified to this Messianic destiny, but more critically they believed that most of these old
laws were "purported to keep Israel aloof from other children
of God," were reflective of "temple sacerdotalism," and had
lost all significance. Their retention in public service or private practice was charged to be "superstitious, a degradation
of Jewish religiosity and piety."

In his annual conference message to the Central Conference of American Rabbis in 1895, Isaac Mayer Wise interpreted the purpose of the liturgical reforms instituted by Reform Judaism as an effort to make the essence of Judaism
"better known and accessible to the human family for salvation and satisfaction of each and all . . ." Pointing to Ameri-

can Judaism's willingness to embrace all of humankind within its fold, Wise applauded the Conference for allowing proselytes to enter Judaism without subjecting themselves "to the Abrahamidic rite" (circumcision), and removing all racial barriers from Israel's covenant. Said Wise: "(The CCAR) declared not only the equality of all human beings before God and his law in time and eternity, but declared also the inviolable attachment and obedience to the laws of the land and the people of this country as the religious duty of every Israelite."

It is interesting to note that even in these early days there was some demur against this effort to revise the liturgy so broadly as to cause Judaism to lose its particularity. In a sermon given before the Central Conference of American Rabbis in 1902, Rabbi Henry Cohen suggested that American Reform Judaism had gone too far in disposing of the ceremonies and rituals of traditional Judaism. Said Cohen: "Religious principles cannot float in the air disembodied. Christianity arose as a protest against Pharisaism, and yet in both Greek and Roman Catholicism there was developed a ritualism that in elaborateness and minuteness far surpassed the ceremonies of the Pharisees. It is folly to presume that we can dispense altogether with symbolism."

Reform Judaism gained many adherents, but freedom produced a movement chaotic and without coherence. Reform Jewish leaders recognized, therefore, that some kind of national organization was required. In this the Reform Jewish leaders were engaged in an effort similar to that of their Christian colleagues. Patterning themselves after the precedents of organized religious life about them, and reflecting the influence and importance of the laity in the movement, the first Reform Jewish institution to be created was the Union of

American Hebrew Congregations in 1873, consisting of 28 congregations. The Hebrew Union College was then established in Cincinnati in 1875 and finally a Central Conference of American Rabbis with Isaac Mayer Wise as first President, was organized in 1889 with 90 rabbis in attendance.

Each of these organizations had hoped to be representative of all of the Jews in the United States; but the whole spirit of this country, emphasizing nonconformity and individualism, precluded that possibility. Even Reform rabbis and congregations refused to give wholehearted support to their own coordinated institutions. An effort was made in the early 1900's, for example, to develop an even more centralized authoritative agency for American Jews. It was rejected. The persuasive arguments reflected the spirit of American voluntarism. It was held that there "was no necessity of pursuing such centralizing tendencies in American Israel." The rabbis rejected any attempt "to bring about a uniform Israel in matters exclusively religious, matters that should forever be left to the individual." Rabbi Bernhard Felsenthal characterized the conflict as one between "the dominion of an intelligent, democratic individualism and the dominion of an obscure and spirit-killing clericalism." He branded the proposal for an authoritative synod as "un-American."

Commenting upon this early experience, CCAR President Rabbi Joseph Silverman, in 1914, described the CCAR by saying:

> It possesses all of the merits of a synod without creating the evil of an autocratic ecclesiastical authority. The very fact that the members of the Conference are not bound by any of its decisions, but the public sentiment demands a justification from those who refuse to accept

them, acts as a check upon refusal dictated merely by whim and arbitrariness. This is an unrecorded achievement and has a high moral value.

An interesting phenomenon during this period, also, was the rise of benevolent, fraternal, and cultural societies not necessarily related to church or synagogue. Alexis de Toqueville in 1830 had remarked: "In no country in this world has the principle of association been more successfully used or more unsparingly applied to the multitude of different objects, than in America." In Europe, however, operating within the tight confines of the Jewish community, such organizations had always been interpenetrated with religious influences, whereas in America they began to assume a secular character. By definition in Protestant America, with its pattern of church-state separation, that which was not directly under clerical or church control was of the secular order—even though the purposes and the values of the institution reflected the influence of religion.

The large influx of German refugees required social services beyond that of the capacity of the synagogues in this country. Thus there emerged free-loan societies, and fraternal orders offering health and death benefits. By 1860 five major national, fraternal organizations had been formed, such as B'nai B'rith with 50 lodges, orphanages, and other philanthropies, the Independent Order of the Sons of Abraham, Free Sons of Israel. Jewish hospitals were established in New York, Chicago, and Cincinnati. In Philadelphia a United Hebrew Charity was formed in 1869 and another in New York in 1874. YMHAs, modeled after the YMCA, also appeared. The first was in Baltimore in 1854, and by 1880 there were fifty in existence. In 1902 Rabbi Leo M. Franklin, in a report before the Central Conference of American Rabbis, said: "It is the curse of our day that the club and not the synagogue has become the center of our life." He explained that the social and social welfare functions of the Jewish community were being served by other organizations, whereas at that time "the temple opened its door but only once or twice a week."

In this promised land, American Jews quickly achieved positions of economic and political power; but then, the violent reaction of Protestants to Catholic immigration forced Jews to realize that many Americans considered this country a Christian (Protestant) nation. With the haunting recollection that religious imperialism had always before involved civil disabilities for dissenters, Jews threw their political energies into the support of civil rights for Catholics. They opposed nativism, in all its forms, and insisted on complete separation of church and state. They also attacked anti-Semitism with a new aggressiveness. Thus opened a new chapter in the Jewish experience of America.

The Immigration and Experiences of Eastern European Jews

America provided a haven of refuge for more than two million Jews who fled to these shores between 1881 and 1914. The Jews of Eastern Europe, unlike their Western European coreligionists, had never experienced political freedom. Russia had withstood the onslaught of the Napoleonic Revolution but the totalitarian tyranny of the tzars became evermore oppressive when cracks in the wall inevitably appeared; for no nation could hold off forever emancipation and enlightenment, science and capitalistic industrialization, the consequences of which were to intensify the demand for political freedom and a more humane share of the productivity of labor.

The achievement of that freedom was delayed, as we have seen, for a period as the Tzarist government, in league with a reactionary church, initiated pogroms against Jews and sought to identify revolution for freedom as a Jewish conspiracy against Holy Russia.

Jewish flight from the wretched conditions of life in Russia, however, was but a small trickle in a total immigration of more than 22 million Old World refugees who sought the haven of these shores. America, said the Jewish poet Emma Lazarus, is the "mother of exiles." But whereas other immigrants included a high percentage of men who were seeking their fortune here first before sending for their families or returning to their former homelands—almost one third of all non-Jewish immigrants to America between 1908 to 1914 returned to their homes—the Jews came to America to stay. Entire families and villages spilled out of one boat after another.

There was a significant nativist reaction in the United States against the alleged threat to the American way of life from these foreign immigrants. The first restrictive efforts were directed particularly against the Catholics.

This antagonism toward the Catholic aliens, however, was soon directed against the Jewish immigrants as well, and within the Protestant underground there circulated tracts charging a Jewish conspiracy to destroy American democratic institutions. Political efforts were made to develop a new immigration law that would be weighted in favor of white Anglo-Saxon Protestant immigrants. The Central Conference of American Rabbis assumed leadership in the struggle to oppose the nativists and to keep wide open America's gates. In an address before the Central Conference of American Rabbis in 1904, Rabbi A. Hirschberg confessed that while restrictive legislation would materially lessen the difficulties and perplexing intricacies of the Jew's own problems, nevertheless, he asserted, "we must, if we are to be true to our teachings, make a determined fight for the admission of these immigrants." Hirschberg called upon the Reform rabbis "to correct erroneous impressions" concerning the new immigrants, and "to help make America accessible to all our oppressed brothers in foreign lands as our first and immediate duty."

America's Reform Jews also tried to help the Eastern European Jews become Americanized. The Hebrew Sheltering and Immigrant Aid Society, HIAS, provided shelter, sustenance, located friends and relatives, and offered vocational training. The Jewish Agricultural and Industrial Aid Society that functioned until 1922 attempted "to relieve the prevailing conditions in our ghettos" and helped the immigrants find quarters in the interior of America. The National Council of Jewish Women concerned itself particularly with the needs of the immigrant women; and the YMHAs and settlement houses, many of them financed and supported by Reform Jews, offered courses in English, fostered the creative expression of the newcomers, and tried to introduce them into the culture and life of America.

In this sense, therefore, the Reform Jews contributed to the melting pot theory of American culture, that is, they joined in the effort undertaken by all of America's educational agencies, churches, and civic groups, to hasten the Americanization of immigrants. The binding loyalty that would enable all these diverse ethnic groups to participate in American life

without splintering the social order would be the rapid acquisition of English and their wholehearted commitment to individual freedom and to the democratic process. Since America
was a nation of immigrants, all of whom had been in revolt
against their past, the crucial question was not where a man
came from, but what he was now and what he was going to be
tomorrow; to become American and to contribute to the well-
being of America became the goal around which all other
institutional loyalties and personal involvements were measured. America was ready to accept and incorporate into its
culture the best, the richest of the ethnic inheritance of its
immigrants; but it expected the immigrant, in becoming
American, to shed his cultural particularism except for religion.

This phenomenon of Americanization was not unique
among the Jews. For example, the American hierarchy of the
Roman Catholic Church asserted its authority over all property purchased and maintained by Polish Catholics. But the
Poles refused to accede to this process of Americanization;
they seceded from the Church and founded the Polish National Catholic Church in Scranton, Pennsylvania in 1897.
The American influence on the Catholic Church is evident
also through the writings of such men as Isaac Thomas
Hecker, founder of the Paulist Order, and Cardinal James
Gibbons of Baltimore, both of whom championed the American principle of church-state separation. Associated with
them was the most radical of the Catholic prelates, Archbishop John Ireland of St. Paul, Minnesota. In a sermon delivered in 1899 he said, "The Church of America must be,
of course, as Catholic as even in Jerusalem or Rome; but as
far as her garments assume color from the local atmosphere,
she must be American. Let no one dare paint her brow with a

foreign tint or pin to her mantle foreign linings." Archbishop Ireland opposed the effort to organize a parochial school system—a defense against the Protestant character of America's public school; instead he proposed a system whereby Catholics could attend the public school and then receive their religious instruction before or after school hours in the public school building. In 1899, however, Pope Leo XIII issued a papal letter in response to the teachings of Archbishop Ireland in which he said, "We cannot approve the opinions which some comprise under the head of Americanism . . . for it raises a suspicion that there are some among you who conceive of and desire a Church in America different from that which is in the rest of the world. . . ." The papal letter served to intensify the self-ghettoization of the Catholic Church from the American community; but as we are all well aware, the process of Americanization took place nevertheless.

Finally, after World War II, culminating with the election of John Kennedy to the presidency of the United States, Catholics shed the confines of the ghetto and emerged as full-fledged participants in America's political and social life.

This Americanization process created a crisis for the Eastern European Jewish immigrants. For unlike the French or German Jew, they had never been confronted with the lure of freedom in return for the abandonment of their ethnicity. The Eastern European Jew brought with him to America a rich tradition of Orthodox Jewish faith and devotion to the Yiddish and Hebrew languages. America witnessed, therefore, the growth of traditional synagogues and seminaries, as well as a Yiddish press and theater.

Reform leaders recognized that they would find extreme

resistance from the Eastern European Jews to their American "goyish" (Christian) type of liturgy. CCAR proceedings reveal that some of the rabbis encouraged the Reform movement to embrace more Hebrew in its service and to rediscover new significance in old traditions and symbols, the use of which might strike a responsive chord in the heart of the Eastern European immigrant and at the same time link the American Reform Jew more closely to the religious convictions of his brethren.

Just prior to this major immigration America had developed its public school system. Most Reform temples abandoned their all-day schools. Their children instead went to the public school and attended a Sabbath or Sunday school for two hours a week, a pattern similar to that followed by the Protestants. This meager educational program, however, was hardly satisfactory to Eastern European Jews, who developed instead their own pattern of religious schools, yeshivot and all-day schools.

Many of the Eastern European immigrants were also Zionists. In addition to holding to a belief that the Jewish people would achieve their proper dignity only when reconstituted as a nation in Palestine, they insisted that a Judaism that denied the values and traditions of a corporate peoplehood was a distortion and a travesty. Jewishness, they asserted, embodied more than a faith. It included tastes and smells, ceremonies, the music and sounds of the tradition, all of which spoke of one people and one destiny.

The first attempt to develop a Zionist movement took place in 1896. Although called by Russian Jews, one distinguished American Reform Rabbi, Bernhard Felsenthal, was present. Now in his 75th year, Felsenthal had evidently despaired of the quality of Jewish life that could be obtained by a Jewish minority in America, even under free conditions, and he declared, "We as individual Jews have no special message to deliver to mankind. From Palestine . . . our so-called mission can best be fulfilled." The delegates to this first Zionist meeting in Chicago imitated the pattern of fraternal organizations in the United States with their mysteries and rituals. They called themselves the "Knights of Zion," emulating such American organizations as the Knights of Labor and the Knights of Columbus. Other Reform rabbis broke rank with their movement to support this Zionist effort. These included Rabbis Gustaf Gottheil of New York, Maximilian Heller of New Orleans, and Solomon Freehof of Pittsburgh.

A Federation of American Zionists was born in New York in 1898. Rabbis Stephen S. Wise, and later Judah Magnes, distinguished Reform leaders, served as secretary to this movement. But in general, the Zionists were opposed by Reform rabbis. In 1897 the CCAR resolved totally to disapprove of any attempt for the establishment of a Jewish state. Such attempts, said the rabbis, "show a misunderstanding of Israel's mission, which from the narrow political and national field has been expanded to the promotion among the whole human race of the broad and universalistic religion first proclaimed by Jewish prophets." The CCAR asserted that the effort of the Zionists to maintain an ethnic individuality "infinitely harms our Jewish brethren where they are still persecuted by confirming the assertion of their enemies that the Jews are foreigners in the countries in which they are at home." In a slashing attack on Zionism delivered at the CCAR convention in 1899, Rabbi Henry Berkowitz charged that Zionism branded as hopeless the condition of Jews throughout Europe. Said Rabbi Berkowitz, "I have not lost faith in the triumph of justice in the world. Furthermore," he added, "the ultimate end and aim of our history is the maintenance of Jews. Judaism has preserved itself thus far because of the power of its ideals and the inspiration of its precepts. These are eternal and superior to race or nationality . . . It is a sad blunder which Zionism here commits to urge upon the Jews to draw apart on racial lines."

In 1906 the president of the CCAR, Rabbi Joseph Stolz, warned,

> Our Judaism is our justification for distinctiveness in the eyes of the state, and in the eyes of our fellow men this is beyond all question a perfectly legitimate justification. But should we make anything else than our religion the line of cleavage from our non-Jewish fellow citizens, we would be putting into the mouths of others an excuse for anti-Semitism and would be giving our enemies an opportunity to charge us with an unwillingness to assimilate and to impute unto us the desire of creating a state within a state.

In defense of Zionism, Professor C. Levias of the Hebrew Union College mocked this commitment to "an imaginary universality of belief." He said,

> The road to messianic times lies rather in the development of the various groups of mankind along the innate peculiarities and natural idiosyncracies of the greatest possible perfection that each of them is capable of obtaining . . . a cosmopolitan religion is an impossibility . . . the watchword a "common humanity" is but a meaningless jingle . . . religion is not a bundle of intellec-

tual ideas but a complex phenomenon of a given nation's soul-life which must disappear with the disappearance of the people. Without Jews there can be no Judaism.

Reform Judaism was not to divest itself of hostility to Zionism until the tragic destruction of the Jewish community during the Nazi period made necessary the establishment of a place of refuge in Palestine. But perhaps even more significant was the fact that as Eastern European Jews made their way into American society and joined the ranks of Reform Judaism, they inspired it to a deeper appreciation of the meaning and beauty of the cultural symbols and ceremonies of traditional religious practice. Without abandoning its commitment to an understanding of the ideals of Judaism in universal terms, the Reform Jew began to recognize the emotional warmth and beauty of his particularistic traditions and of his link with fellow Jews throughout the world. Giving expression to this new understanding, Rabbi Barnett Brickner in 1932, in an address before the CCAR said,

I believe that the synthesis between Reform Judaism and Jewish nationalism is both a logical and emotional necessity. The two must not . . . be kept apart any longer. Jewish nationalism needs the dynamic of religion for its motivation and power, and Reform needs the whole household of Israel for its congregation . . . If the Jewish community become a church, and we should live in every respect like our neighbors excepting in our profession of ethical monotheism, then by the judgment of every social thinker the survival of the church itself would be jeopardized . . . Our experience in America . . . with the philosophy that we are Jews by religion only, has demonstrated that wherever it has been rigorously taught and adhered to it has led to assimilation. And were it not for the fact that despite this profession we maintain special philanthropies, a distinctive social life of our own, and develop all the other institutions of community—it is doubtful whether even our temple would have survived.

Sociologists in this most recent period have pointed out that while there is a tendency among all Americans to give up their ethnic distinctiveness for a religious pluralism, Jews more than any others maintain a communality of interest that distinguishes them from other religious groups. In a significant way, Rabbi Brickner's assertion has come true, for these studies also indicate the Jews are less attentive to their ritualistic religious duties than any other of America's religions, but nevertheless Jewish values, insights, and understandings continue to be communicated in the communality of Jewish expression through its various community relations organizations, educational and service clubs, social welfare and cultural enterprises, many of which of course find their leadership from among the religious community.

Early in the 1930's such philosophers as Louis Adamack, John Dewey, and Horace Kallen argued that the impulse to eliminate otherness is a reflection of immaturity. The American idea is enriched by pluralism," said Kallen. But just when the Reform Rabbis recognized that assimilation ought not be the end of the Americanization process and that the immigrant was capable of giving as well as taking, the melting pot had already worked its damage. The National Resources Committee in 1938 sadly observed: "There is a natural tendency toward the assimilation of diverse cultures in some communities. It is quite likely that this process has been forced too rapidly in the United States, with results that have been personally and socially injurious."

Eastern European Socialism and Reform Jew's Social Action

Among the Eastern European immigrants there were also many who were socialists. They had been part of the liberal revolutionary effort inside of Russia. While devoted to Yiddish, and concerned for the maintenance of cultural ties to the Jewish community, they had rejected the rigid patterns of Orthodox religion, the only kind they had experienced in Russia. In America, these Jews found that although they were guaranteed political freedom, conditions of servitude prevailed in the sweatshop factories that welcomed them, many of which were owned by German Jews.

These socialist Russian Jews eagerly joined the newly developing labor movement in the United States, and by 1888 a United Hebrew Trades Organization was in existence. Jewish affiliates were to be found among the bakers, waiters, printers, teamsters, furriers, and particularly from the needle trades there emerged two great unions, the International Ladies Garment Workers Union, and the Amalgamated Clothing Workers of America.

Strikes called by these latter organizations witnessed settlements that set a pace for the whole labor movement. In 1910 a protocol of peace between the ILGWU and management, written under the guidance of a Boston lawyer named Louis Brandeis (later to become a Justice of the Supreme Court), set up a permanent board of arbitration that has held firm to this day as an effective means of settling industrial conflicts.

The Amalgamated also experimented with social services for its members. It has built cooperative apartment houses, organized education and recreational programs, developed unemployment insurance, medical and health programs and pension plans, all in advance of governmental efforts in these areas.

In contrast to the general labor movement that at first had concerned itself only with the limited benefits required to ease their condition of work, and had avoided aligning itself with any political program of economic reconstruction, the Jewish labor leaders saw "the labor movement as an instrument for hastening the redemption of mankind." They were "ardent advocates of radical social programs and universal panaceas."

It must be noted that the Jewish socialists were zealously anti-Communists, and despite an initial success among some Jews in the United States, the number of Jewish Communists dwindled as the Jews entered the middle class and absorbed an American resistance to any form of political radicalism.

The contribution of the Reform movement to the economic and political situation in the United States during this period is pale when contrasted to the effective action of the Jewish socialists and the Jewish labor movement, which drew its strength from the Eastern European immigrants. The Reform temple was in the decisive control of the wealthy American Jew, and the Reform rabbi only hesitatingly involved himself in any radical prescription for social and legislative change. If the Reform rabbinate lagged far behind the Eastern European socialist Jew, they trailed as well far behind those liberal Protestant churchmen who had involved themselves in the development of the "Social Gospel" movement.

America's economic system of laissez-faire capitalism reached its peak of achievement by the 1880's. "It lingered on," points out Max Lerner, "through the support of the on-rush of immigrants who were driven hard and often exploited as workers, but who fed on the dream of success and never lost their sense of its possibility."

Nevertheless, between 1880 and 1920 America's industrialists demonstrated a shocking lack of sensitivity for the plight of the worker in the new mass production industries. In response to the laborer's desperate cry of human need, a new set of economic theories came to the fore. These were given moral support and religious foundation in the Protestant-stimulated Social Gospel Movement. The morality of the American Christian was shocked by the corruption of the capitalist barons of this country and disclosures of the tie-in between business management and the city bosses. The use of civic power by economic overlords to repress the poor evoked religious indignation. Significant also was the fact that America's rural economy was becoming industrial. By 1919 the major corporations employed 86% of all wage earners, maintaining them in substandard labor conditions. Church leaders, therefore, began to call upon federal and state governments to take on a variety of functions never dreamed of in the philosophy of a naturally functioning economic order. These included the regulation of railroads, banks, business and labor, the establishment of working hours and conditions of employment. As early as 1888, James Bryce in his *American Commonwealth* noted that while Americans had the phantasy of living under a system of laissez-faire, they were actually living under one in which the government was extending its intervention "into ever widening fields."

Although Samuel Gompers in 1898 wrote: "My associates have come to look upon the church and the ministry as the apologists and defenders of the wrongs committed against the interests of the people," there were many churchmen who proposed radical change in the economic system. St. George's Episcopal Church in New York between 1883 and 1889 spent over $2,000,000 for philanthropic purposes. Courses were conducted in the church on industrial relations. The Congregational Barclay Temple in Boston and the Philadelphia Baptist Temple distinguished themselves by setting up sewing glasses, manual training courses, day nurseries, and social clubs. In 1894 those churches that had been involved in an effort to bring about a change in social economic conditions organized themselves into an Institutional Church League to coordinate their activities. They promised "to open the church doors every day and all the days, to provide free seats for a plurality of Christian workers, to involve all church members in a ministry to all the community, to educational reform, and to all philanthropic channels." The YMCA expanded its operation, as did the Salvation Army in an effort to bring social services to the poor immigrants. Washington Gladden, George D. Herron, and Walter Rauschenbusch were distinguished Protestant leaders in their churches' forceful attack on capitalism. Said Rauschenbusch: "Competitive commerce exalts selfishness to the dignity of a moral principle. It pits men against one another in a gladiatorial game in which there is no mercy and in which 90% of the combatants finally strew the arena."

The Methodist, Baptist, Congregational, Presbyterian, Disciple, and Episcopalian churches all adopted social creeds between 1901 and 1908. They established agencies to put their creeds into practice. The Federal Council of Churches in 1908 issued a social creed of the churches which was again revised in 1912, urging equal rights for all men, uniform divorce laws, child labor laws, old age benefits, labor arbitration, one day of rest weekly, reduction of working hours, and "the application of Christian principles to the acquisition and use of property." It was not until 1918 that the CCAR adopted a statement on social justice which was reworked, revised, debated, and chewed over until in 1928 a program of 17 extended paragraphs was adopted which placed the CCAR in support of that program of social and economic change which the major Protestant denominations of America had adopted a decade before.

Nevertheless, the involvement of the CCAR was not insignificant and there were bright moments that should be remembered. As early as 1900, for example, Rabbi Charles S. Levy took the occasion to comment on the changing attitudes towards the concept of individualism. Acknowledging the contribution of the idea of individual liberty with its beneficent result in constitutional government, public education, and the liberalism of religion, Rabbi Levy asserted nevertheless:

The battles in the fields of industry, commerce, and handicrafts went to the strong. The race and the struggle for things material went to the swift. The temple of the 19th-century civilization was built on the ruins of the seventeen previous centuries without using as a cement the cooperative mixtures of 'one for all and all for one' . . . Individualism is the rare incense that needs the leavening effect of the idea of brotherhood to give it permanent value. Our century proved that all men are not born free and equal, neither physically nor mentally nor morally. The maimed, the halt and the blind in body, mind, and soul are not on a par with the sound, the swift, and the sane. They are free only in their consent to be governed and equal before the administration of justice alone. Cooperation, not competition; expansion, not seclusion; association, not isolation; international congresses of peace and arbitration, not the self-righteous, solitary tribunals of lowly governments; parliaments of religion, not conferences of single denominations; profit-sharing industries, not proprietary privileges; combinations of labor and capital, not individual work and investment; the federation of men, not the separation of the human spirit—these are now the "open sesames" that lead to the promised land flowing with the milk and honey of the ages to come. New times, new duties make the ancient truths untrue. Infant industries need the fostering protection of the governments, helpless man needs the upbuilding protection of society.

In 1907 the newly established Free Synagogue of Rabbi Steven S. Wise built into its organization a social service department similar to that of some of the Protestant churches in New York City. Explaining the program in his bulletin, Rabbi Wise pointed out that 45% of the temple's budget would be allocated to social service. "Not charity, but social service, building upon the rock of social justice will be the watchword of the Free Synagogue. The essential thing in the religion of Israel . . . is to quicken and keep alive the social conscience, to strengthen and to make indissoluble the social bond." The Free Synagogue's Social Welfare Department inaugurated a project with Bellevue Hospital whose Social Service Department had confessed itself as "absolutely incapable of dealing with Jewish patients because of their alien language, religion, customs, and habits." They also experimented with a program in mental hygiene. In those days 20% of the patients admitted to Bellevue Psychopathic Ward were Jewish outpatient clinics and they received hospitable and friendly care from fellow coreligionists in the Free Synagogue's Social Welfare Department.

In 1909 the CCAR devoted a full symposium to the question of the religion and the problems of the working man. The division within the Reform rabbinate is apparent in the debate that took place during that time. Rabbi Solomon Foster scorned the Christian churches who had set themselves to the task "of solving the vexing problem" of the laborer, and asserted,

> Although the church has involved itself in a ministry of preaching in factories, sitting in labor conventions, signing petitions of industrial reforms, agitating for sanitary factories and protected machinery, better housing conditions and the like, the church as a church has not recorded a single triumph of consequence in its work among the wage earners. It is impossible for the synagogue to master the necessary details of a great economic problem to warrant the attempt to solve it . . . The synagogue must stand near to assist as far as possible that the rules of the contest, justice, righteousness, and kindliness shall not be ignored by either party. But if in its official capacity it were to turn to champion the cause of the laboring man against his employer, simply by reason of its inability to speak with authority on any subject outside of religion, it would not at all be unlikely that a temporary victory by the synagogue would become ultimately a graveyard and a danger to the very interests of the class it had sought to help.

In bitter response, Rabbi Sidney Harris countered at that CCAR convention saying:

> Some will say we should not meddle with labor questions, that it is not part of our duty. They say further that we really know nothing about the economic, technical, and sociological issues involved. If we do not know these issues intimately, then it is time we did. More important it is that we should study the problems of the working men around us than the literature in obscure tongues and in musty tones of a thousand years ago. We should stand on the side of the working man because he is often a submerged class and our place is by the side of the submerged class; that is . . . our motif.

The CCAR in 1906 concerned itself with national marriage and divorce legislation, in 1908 with child labor, in 1911 with the problems of labor arbitration, in 1913 with higher wages for labor. It cooperated with the Committee on Good Will of the Federal Council of Churches and the National Catholic Welfare Conference in efforts to arbitrate industrial conflict, but resistance to profound involvement in the particular problems of social living continued to exist within the Reform rabbinate. As late as 1919, in an essay entitled "The Synagogue, the War, and the Days Beyond," Horace J. Wolf, calling upon the synagogue to become "a militant agent for social justice," acknowledged that the interpretation of this function of the synagogue will meet with opposition. "There will be those," he said, "who will maintain that the synagogue should busy itself with personal righteousness rather than social improvement, with theological speculation rather than social transgressions." Wolf himself hedged his own demand for action by suggesting "I do not plead that the synagogue should become a class institution nor that it should sponsor any specific economic scheme. Its criticisms of existing social wrongs should be from the moral rather than the economic and its approach from high spiritual ground rather than the low plane of controversial economics."

The truth is, of course, that if economic social change is to take place, the impact and force of moral decision must be brought to bear upon the specific alternatives that are available. Thus this criticism leveled by Rabbi Max Heller against the earliest efforts of the CCAR's Commission on Social Justice to give support to a systematic program of social change by generalized resolution-making: "The statement of the Commission on Social Justice skims the surface and is to the average student of prevailing conditions neither informing nor illuminating. They present in each case a kind of précis of the problem and leave unstated the principal difficulties as well as the most promising remedies and solutions. One of these statements is a sermon rather than a practical survey."

By 1931, however, when America had suffered through the depression and the reforms of the New Deal were only on the horizon, Rabbi Morris Newfield in his presidential message before the CCAR, gave expression to the Conference's now unquestioned endorsement of economic liberal reform. "Even more loudly we protest," he said, "against a system which in the most approved laissez-faire fashion engenders periodically a most tragic culmination of moderate, but continuous unemployment conditions." The Commission on Social Justice in that year asserted: "The government, amid the inactivity or impotence of private industry, must act in a manner to stimulate industry and cause employment." The Commission called for a two to three billion dollar public works program, for increased taxation from income in higher brackets, for federal support of state and local relief funds, for compulsory unemployment insurance "and for a more equitable distribution of the profits of industry through wage increases."

In 1932 Rabbi Barnett Brickner, pleaded with the rabbis to involve themselves deeply in the work of social change. "In this Conference," he said, "we have in the main been content with adopting radical platforms about social justice, but how far have any of us permitted ourselves to commit our very all to its achievement? Some of us say that the church and temple have no right to take sides in the social and economic struggle, that their function is rather to be powerhouses of inspiration . . . but I ask, whoever saw a powerhouse whose electrical energy was not connected by wires to some machine designed to do a certain task . . ." Again in 1939, Rabbi Samuel H. Goldenson, in a Conference address entitled "The Democratic Implications of Jewish Moral and Spiritual Thinking" confessed: "Unfortunately our synagogues are too much identified with and too frequently under the control of only the well-to-do members of our congregations. We, who insist upon the moral values of democracy, should not rest until remedies are found."

Finally, in June 1964, in a statement entitled "The Rabbi and the Political Process," a response to congregants who had criticized Reform rabbis for their political outspokenness, the CCAR affirmed the rabbi's right and obligation to exercise political responsibility as a citizen and as a moral teacher. This statement said,

Politics is the primary means through which a democratic society determines its nature and purposes. If, as social scientists have discovered, the most formative influence in the life of an individual is the overall environment, then the rabbi who seeks to affect the character of his congregants must seek to affect the character of the environment in which they live. In general, the rabbi addresses himself to issues and not to personalities or to parties in politics, but at crucial times in the life of a community or nation and when in his judgment it is deemed necessary, the rabbi should be free to take a public position in political campaigns.

When in 1932 the Rabbinical Assembly of Conservative Synagogues organized its Social Action Commission, it confessed:

It is clear that in this area the Reform and Conservative rabbis follow rather than lead the Jewish community, and this is not the case in some Protestant denominations, where the ministers, even if not leaders on social attitudes, generally expressed social attitudes in advance of their parishioners . . . Jewish social attitudes derive more from 19th-century liberalism and socialism than the Hebrew prophets . . . It is not easy to see in present-day Jewish social attitudes the heritage of the Jewish religion.

Despite a tardy acceptance of social responsibility it is clear at this point that Reform rabbis have taken a significant lead in the cause of social action and that Jews in particular stand in the forefront of the struggle for social righteousness in our country. It was as late as 1932 that the CCAR first expressed "deep concern with and a condemnation of conditions . . . which seemed to offer evidence of the inability of the Negro to secure economic or civil justice." Today, however, rabbis are among those who have participated in sit-ins, freedom rides, and the campaign of sensitive white leaders to provide Negroes with the right to vote. The Reform movement's Department of Social Action in particular has led the way in American Judaism by its participation in commissions on religion and race throughout the country and in testimony before Congress on significant legislative matters. Nevertheless, there remain significant weaknesses in its organizational efforts in this regard. The Social Action Department itself is handicapped with a lack of personnel and adequate resources.

The Battle Against Anti-Semitism

The failure of the CCAR to follow through with a significant commitment of personnel and resources for programmatic achievement in its area of social concern, is particularly evident in the history of the CCAR's involvement in the fight against prejudice and anti-Semitism in the United States.

Anti-Semitism has always existed in the United States. To begin with, it is the inevitable inheritance of any Christian civilization. As we have already seen in Chapter 2, for 1500 years Christianity had encouraged Jew-hatred and justified oppressive patterns of political, economic, and social discrimination by its teaching that the Jews were a deicide people, rejected by God, condemned to servitude, and that Judaism was a degenerate religion. Such teachings, of course, are a mockery of true Christianity. They distort the Gospels, and feed on superstition and ignorance. Fortunately for the Jews throughout our history, there have been Christians, made compassionate by their faith, who have stood firm against anti-Semitism and have heroically sought justice for the Jew.

As long as the American frontier remained open and America kept faith with its promise "to give bigotry no sanction," the Jew remained secure. There were isolated incidents, such as General Grant's order Number 11 during the Civil War banning Jewish traders from the battlefields, and the refusal in 1877 of the Grand Union Hotel to admit the celebrated Jewish public figure Joseph Seligman, and the slanderous charge of New York's Police Commissioner in 1908 that the Russians (Jews) contributed 50% of the city's criminals. But Jews were never seriously threatened in their political status or in their civil rights. Nevertheless, the leadership of the CCAR refused to be silent about the growth of social anti-Semitism.

As early as 1905 Rabbi Joseph Krauskopf, noting that hotel exclusion of Jews had grown from "one summer hotel in 1877 to hundreds in 1905, and from hotels this restriction has spread to schools, clubs, fraternities, and the like," asserted: "The undreamed of a generation ago has almost become a common occurrence in our day . . . the humiliation which this exclusion has inflicted upon our people has been especially distressing because of the conviction that the insult is as basely cruel as it is fundamentally un-American." He noted that for almost a quarter of a century such anti-Semitism had been treated with sound contempt. We have acted on the principle, he said, that to notice such indignities is to give them an importance they little deserve. Rabbi Krauskopf called for an end of that policy. "Why should the world think better of us than it does when in Sabbath school and in church it hears the Jew accursed and in social life it sees the Jew ostracized and not a Jew rising publicly and vigorously to protest against these utterly groundless charges and these unwarranted exclusions." Krauskopf recommended that a standing committee be constituted to investigate the most effective measures for the checking and ultimate suppression of such anti-Semitism and to publish the results of its studies and enquiries for free distribution wherever and whenever required.

Five years later the CCAR Committee on Church-State Relations, preceding the Anti-Defamation League of B'nai B'rith by some years, engaged in a campaign to discourage "lampooning of the Jew on the stage" and recommended that whenever the word Jew is applied to malefactors in the local press, members of the CCAR ought to protest against this manifest injustice. The campaign of the CCAR benefited not only the Jew, but the Irish and other immigrants as well. In 1911 Alex Pantage, president of the large chain of theaters and show houses across the land, assured the leadership of the CCAR "we have notified all our houses to eliminate anything objectionable to any race or denomination. That includes the Irish as well as the Jewish character."

The CCAR engaged in the publication of tracts explaining the Jewish holy days for Christian readers. It protested the requirement of the reading of *The Merchant of Venice* for College Board Exams. It protested anti-Semitic songs and statements in the textbooks and music books of the public schools of the United States. But then, without demur, the CCAR gave over leadership in this anti-defamation work to lay-controlled, community relations organizations. By failing to provide adequate funds, resources, and manpower, the CCAR itself, permitted the work of Jewish defense to be separated from the centrality of synagogal and religious concern.

When anti-Semitism in America, therefore, took its most vicious political form with the passage of the restrictive immigration law of 1924 and the emergence of the Ku Klux Klan

and the spread of Nazism, it was not the synagogue organizations, but rather the lay community relations groups that were
prepared and equipped to deal with this threat.

The CCAR cooperated in an initial effort to develop a
National Conference of Christians and Jews that would co-
ordinate the work of America's religious leadership in the
battle against bigotry and prejudice. The original idea for an
interfaith movement against hate had emerged out of the
Federal Council of Churches' study of the Ku Klux Klan at its
convention in Atlanta, Georgia in 1924. Its call for a Committee on Good Will between Jews and Christians was stimulated with a grant of $6,000 from the B'nai B'rith. Work
started in Chicago, Cleveland, Detroit, and St. Louis. Leaders
of the B'nai B'rith, the Central Conference of American
Rabbis, and the Federal Council of Churches joined together
to plan the program. From these meetings emerged the National Conference of Christians and Jews. The CCAR had
earlier established a Committee of Good Will that had been
working with the Federal Council of Churches, but it was
impossible to achieve any constructive results because of the
inevitable conservatism and delay involved in winning commitment from entire organizations and denominations. The
NCCJ, an organization of religiously committed individuals,
seemed a suitable substitute. Rabbi Louis Wolsey and Rabbi
Abba Hillel Silver represented the CCAR in these negotiations and provided important leadership to the NCCJ.
Reform laymen, such as Roger William Strauss and Arthur
Sulzberger, representing the Union of American Hebrew
Congregations, were among the earliest co-chairmen, and
provided the NCCJ with significant initial financial gifts. In
1932 the CCAR officially pledged its moral support to the

NCCJ, but by 1940 there was a disappointment registered within the CCAR at the "growing staleness of the good will devices used by the NCCJ." Rabbi Emile Leipziger in an address before the CCAR indicated that the methods of the NCCJ, its Brotherhood Week Program, and its Interfaith team of speakers, were "designed only to scratch the surface of the problem of good neighborliness. Their efforts," he said, "fail to play up aspects of economic and social problems as the cause of racial and religious ill will."

The most significant work in cooperation with Christian groups in the rewriting and revision of church-school texts, in the development of joint social action programs against anti-Semitism, and in response to a growing concern on the part of the Catholic Church for its role in the shaping of the world, has taken place through a rabbinical leadership within the ranks of the Anti-Defamation League and the American Jewish Committee. The pioneer rabbis in both of these organizations were members of the CCAR—Rabbi Arthur Gilbert and Morris Kertzer. Only belatedly has the UAHC organized a Commission on Interfaith Relations whose single executive finds himself overwhelmed with an abundance of responsibility.

Defining the Relations of Church and State

Reform Judaism's most significant contribution to social theory in the United States is to be found in the work of its Church-State Committee and in its effort to define the relationship of church and state in America's pluralistic society. As early as 1904, long before other religious groups were aware of the significance of this issue, the CCAR involved itself in a battle against sectarianism in public institutions. In an address before the CCAR Rabbi Joseph Krauskopf asserted:

> As American citizens and in the name of American citizens of Jewish and non-Jewish persuasion, we must protest against the sectarianizing of our public schools. As profoundly as we respect the Christian creed and as sacredly as we venerate the Bible, and as heartily as we approve of the study of the Bible as literature in connection with the study of classical literature, so strenuously must we oppose their introduction for religious purposes into institutions which are maintained by the Commonwealth. Respectfully, but emphatically, we must say to all who trespass upon our citizenship rights in public institutions: Have all the Christianity you wish, cherish it as much as you can, enthrone it in your church, but keep it from public schools. Let us be Protestants or Catholics, agnostics or Jews in our churches or homes; in our public institutions, however, let us be Americans.

Rabbi Krauskopf recommended a Conference standing committee of five, whose duty it would be to gather whatever literature there exists on the illegality and danger of sectarianism in the public schools and in other public institutions. The very next year that committee issued a report in which it cautioned the Jew against initiating legal test cases with regard to sectarian practices in the public schools. "Defeat in such matters is so baneful that the risk of it had rather not be incurred. It is best that we concentrate our efforts upon the education of public opinion on this very important subject." The CCAR then engaged in a most significant program of public education. Its findings in the early 1900's still serve as guide and model to reasoned considerations of issues by rabbinical and educational leaders in our own day. For ex-ample, in 1909 the CCAR committee queried the American Reform rabbis on the wisdom of the establishment of a course of ethics or morals for the public schools of the United States: Of 57 who returned answers, 19 thought such courses would be advisable; three urged it as a study along with civics; five of the 19 added the proviso that such courses would be accepta-ble if sectarian coloring could be prevented; but 37 deemed such courses inadvisable, some because they were sure that sectarian bias could not be eliminated from such teaching, some because they felt that ethics should never be separated from religious teaching, some because teachers, prepared as they were, could not adequately teach so important and deli-cate a subject; but most significantly, most of those who urged the inadvisability of such a set course in ethics or morality in the public schools, stated that these subjects are inherent in all school studies and that it only requires the true teacher to suggest them to the pupil where intrinsic to the child's experi-ence in the public school. Education in character should be the undercurrent in all teaching, asserted the rabbis, a view-point maintained today by educational leaders with greater vigor than ever before.

Rabbi Tobias Schonfarber in 1911, in a discussion on moral training in the schools, asserted:

Even though ethics are not definitely and directly taught, it would be a libel to label our public schools, as is sometimes done by narrow credalists, as godless and atheistic ... What the child needs in the school as well as in the home is not so much ethical instruction as it is

moral atmosphere, contact with morality in action . . .
One Horace Mann is worth more than all the didactic
moral instruction and all the textbooks on morality.

Many of the rabbis were uneasy, however, at what they
understood to be the negative position of the CCAR in its
opposition to Bible reading, Christmas and holiday celebrations in the public school, and now ethical instruction in the
public school. A compromise solution in 1916 and 1917,
therefore, was to support the initial proposals for released
time, which provided that children might be excused from the
public school to receive their religious instruction during the
school day, but outside of the school property. In a resolution
adopted at that time, the Chairman of the Church-State
Committee called upon the Conference at that time not to
content itself "merely with the negative attitude of insisting
upon the complete separation of church and state, but it
should whenever it can, constructively and helpfully meet all
efforts made for the improvement of ethical and religious instruction in the nation." By 1940, however, the CCAR recognized that the program of released time had been much
abused throughout the United States. Schools were involved
in the recruiting of students for the released time classes, children were separated off according to religion, those who refused to take their released time classes were often humiliated
and found themselves with nothing but "busy work" to do,
and most importantly, in many communities the released time
classes were conducted right on school property with no provision made for the dissenter. Thus in 1940 Rabbi Emile
Leipziger asserted: ". . . even the most seemingly innocuous
project of released time cannot be practically applied without
danger of becoming an opening wedge for violation of the

American principle of Church-State separation." In 1941 the CCAR resolved that it preferred the shortening of the school day rather than released time. This dismissal time would enable parents and leaders of religion independently of the school to provide for the religious instruction they deemed essential without involvement of the instrumentality of the public school in support of religious education.

In 1939 the CCAR vigorously came to the defense of the Jehovah Witnesses and attacked state laws that compelled the saluting of the American flag. Said the Church-State Committee:

> This law is deliberately aimed at the religious sect known as Jehovah Witnesses who believe that saluting the flag is a form of idolatry and, therefore, prohibited by their religious convictions. . . . This law provides in effect for a form of persecution by the state of a religious minority of our country. This is repugnant to all Americans who believe ardently in our traditional tolerance between church and state.

Thus the CCAR in this issue as in other church-state issues, anticipated the ultimate moral decision that would be rendered by the Supreme Court in support of freedom of conscience and the separation principle. In the wording of this historic resolution the CCAR attempted to make clear to the American people that it was not supporting any effort "to dereligionize American society."

In attempting to define the Conferences's own definition of the meaning of church-state separation, Reform rabbis in 1941 anticipated the legal doctrine that would ultimately be made part of the law of the United States. Said the Church-

State Committee: "The doctrine of separation of church and state in our country has meant that all religious bodies have an equal status before the law. The state is to be free from any ecclesiastical domination. The state respects all faiths, but it supports none. The state is not permitted in our democracy to institutionalize any form of religion." On the other hand, said the CCAR Committee, "On those occasions when civic and patriotic functions require a religious endorsement or dignity, all religious groups are to be respected and represented." The CCAR therefore, was not opposing those civic and patriotic exercises during which reference to this nation's existence under God was to be made. It distinguished between those ceremonies and rituals of American life that have become part of our national heritage and represent our civic consensus as against those practices that are clearly sectarian.

The Committee suggested that religious influence could make itself felt in America through "the interpenetration resulting from the actions of religiously motivated individuals rather than providing the institutionalized church with some national favor or power." Said the report:

Religion is a way of life that is definitely concerned with the decrees and spirit and philosophy of our government. . . . Religion is vitally concerned with the form that the state takes and with the kind of educational training to which youth are subjected. Otherwise we may be unwitting partners in laying conditions that will inevitably lead to our ruin. Character and conscience must be developed in the life of the nation . . . Moral law is imperative and must be applied to our society. We cannot accept the false position that religion is concerned only with devotional worship and its correlated duties while it is the state that determines the social, economic, and political values and purposes of the people.

The Committee called upon all religious bodies to unite in an emphasis on moral ideals, religious principles, and ethical truths in the private lives of America's citizens. Without relaxing in any way "our efforts to keep dogmatic sectarianism out of our schools," the Committee called upon religious leaders and educators to encourage a positive program of moral instruction such as respect for human personality, the sacredness of human life, the love of neighbor in America's public schools. "The outer unity of our democratic structure will crumble," warned the Committee, "if we do not provide an inner unity of our common life's ideals."

Reform Judaism Influences the Pattern of All Jewish Denominations In America

Although Reform Judaism did not win the allegiance or support of the vast majority of the new Eastern European immigrants to America, it nevertheless provided patterns of organization and suggested methods of involving men, women, and children in the work of religion that were copied almost to the letter by Conservative and Orthodox Jews. The influx of Russian Jews strengthened Jewish religious life considerably. In 1877 there were 227 congregations in the United States. By 1900, that figure had almost quadrupled. There were now 850 congregations and most of these new synagogues were traditional in orientation.

The Conservative movement organized itself in reaction to Reform Judaism. Its first leader, Isaac Leeser, had been in attendance, in fact, at the first of the rabbinical conferences called by Isaac Mayer Wise, but he was dissatisfied with the reformist tendencies among most of the German rabbis. In cooperation with his successor as rabbi at Mikveh Israel Synagogue in Philadelphia, Rabbi Sabato Morais, he organized the Jewish Theological Seminary in 1886. In 1901 the graduates of the Seminary, following the pattern set by the Reform rabbinate, gathered themselves into a Rabbinical Assembly of America, and then in 1913 a United Synagogue brought together those congregations that followed Conservative ideals.

In New York and then in Chicago the Orthodox Jews at first attempted to develop cohesion around a "Chief Rabbi" who would provide the legal authority of talmudic interpretation and communal leadership such as had prevailed in the ghettos of Europe. The American experience of pluralism and voluntarism, however, prevailed against such an arrangement. The congregations would not hold together nor did the state support the chief rabbi's power as was the case in the Old World. Thus the Orthodox rabbis finally followed the pattern set by Reform and Conservative Jews, and organized themselves first into a Union of Orthodox Rabbis in 1902 without hierarchical structure. Then it supported the development of a Theological Seminary for the training of Orthodox rabbis, from which eventually emerged Yeshivah College, the first Jewish institution of higher learning in the United States. The American graduates of Yeshivah found themselves, however, worlds apart from their original mentors. Their language was English—the mother tongue of European trained rabbis was Yiddish; Yeshivah graduates had an education that included secular studies, whereas the European rabbis had been trained only in the talmudic academy. American trained rabbis were ready to make concessions and change in dress and in liturgical form, applicable to the needs of American cultural standards, to which the Europeans could never agree. Thus, in 1930, a new Orthodox rabbinical body, the Rabbinical Council of America, was organized.

It is significant to note that America's Reform Jews did not look upon the development of the Orthodox and Conservative movements as a threat nor did they even feel themselves in competition. Lay leaders of Reform Judaism whose bond of sympathy overran any form of restrictive denominational loyalty, contributed to the fund of half a million dollars that brought Rabbi Solomon Schecter from England as the first President of the Jewish Theological Seminary. Compasssion both for the physical and religious need of their coreligionists inspired Reform rabbis by 1937 to introduce into their Platform of Principles a new regard for the peoplehood of Israel and a new openness to the restoration of customs and ceremonies that derive from traditional practice.

Concern for a Theology of Judaism

Just as Reform rabbis recognized that the addition of particularistic and traditional symbols and ceremonies gave richer meaning to their existence of Jews, so they realized that they would have to be more critical than they had originally been to the philosophies and theologies then circulating through the sophisticated, intellectual circles of American society in which they lived. In 1912, in an address before the CCAR, entitled "The Spirit of the Age and the Relation to Judaism," Rabbi Harry H. Mayer was able to boast,

Judaism instead of being out of harmony with the new teachings in philosophy, science, and ethics, is less in conflict with them than any other form of religion, nay, supports them and is supported by them . . . There is room in Judaism for every phase of philosophic truth since Judaism is a tireless search for truth in all things . . . Judaism shares with all modern teachers of ethics the contempt which they have for the fine shades of dogma and the finer shades of doctrine. The new ethics is at one with Judaism also in its recognition of the fact that the moral status of man has been steadily improving and that it is a mistake to invest, in our discontent with the present, some period of the past with ideal attributes . . . The new ethics is based on the historically sound assumption that justice has been expanding and will continue to expand until a perfect justice for all is attained. We insist that salvation is only through character. The spirit of the ages is working powerfully for us. We shall keep step in the hastening march of progress . . .

This talk gave expression to a tendency in American religious thought that was just then under attack from a neoorthodox movement in Protestant Christianity. That is, Rabbi Mayer articulated the traditional American impatience with credalism, an emphasis on this-worldly achievement, and revealed a naïve optimism that the processes of evolution would progressively and inevitably bring about a golden age. Such a theological analysis of history came under sharp attack particularly in the 1920's with the teachings of Reinhold Niebuhr. This neoorthodoxy accepted much of the external forms of liberalism, for example its use of biblical criticism and its rejection of biblical literalism, its toleration of a variety of faiths, its intellectual spirit rather than its pietistic, romantic one. Nevertheless, the neo-reform movement demanded a closer attention to theology and theological issues and, more importantly, it raised questions concerning the inevitability of a progressive evolutionary process. Niebuhr emphasized the sinfulness and inadequacy of man. In an illuminating analysis of political issues, he sought to demonstrate the need for faith and for a God-given saving grace if men were to find the strength with which to deal with complex social problems.

A harmonizing "Amen" to some of these tendencies within American Protestantism was to be heard within the CCAR. In 1920 Rabbi William Fineshriber in an address entitled "The Decay of Theology and Popular Religion" pleaded with his colleagues to recognize that a decay of theology had been accompanied by a lessening of faith. Rabbi Fineshriber added:

> The rationalist spirit of the last century and the absorption in material growth and prosperity have further weakened our hold on faith. Like people, like priest. The sermons of the last generation or two are evidence that the clergy spurs the general indifference towards matters theologic . . . History and sociology, more or less diluted, form the favorite themes of our rabbis. Sermons from the Jewish Reform pulpit on the consciousness of the presence of God are not often heard.

Ten years later, in 1930, Rabbi David Lefkowitz in his presidential address was to note that

> a secularism that cannot be disregarded for a moment . . . is creeping over the whole structure of American Jewish life. The synagogue is feeling the tremors that are

shaking the very foundations of the churches. Super-
naturalism and philosophy in religion is again the center
of attack. This time the synagogue is in greater danger
than from any other onslaught, because the weapon of
the attack is so appealing to the Jewish outlook. Human-
ism with its insistence upon man as the center of life,
with its worldly outlook, catches the initial sympathy of
Judaism . . .

Rabbi Lefkowitz noted that some rabbis had been drawn to
this philosophy "so far as to denominate our prayers as so
much poetry and nothing else. The personality of God, which
is the *ikkar* (central teaching) of Judaism, is being either
categorically or implicitly questioned or rather discarded."

With the growth of Nazism, Reform rabbis also heard from
among their ranks echoes of Reinhold Niebuhr's despair over
the ability of man to achieve alone God's Kingdom upon
earth. In 1940 Rabbi Emile Leipziger, speaking to the
CCAR, cried out:

The logic of history leads us to deepest pessimism; so
does the shrieking reality of the present. The Jew is
caught within a vicious circle of his own driving ideals.
Peace has been his mission and in the light of that mission he should speak every word, perform every act that
will keep America from the maelstrom of war. Yet if
America does not add its might to the forces which the
democracies have engaged, freedom and justice may
vanish from the earth.

On the 50th Anniversary of the CCAR Rabbi Max Cur-
rick, recalling the optimistic faith of Rabbi Isaac Mayer Wise,

said consolingly to the Conference: "The mills of God grind slowly, but the end of days is not yet."

Joshua Loth Liebman, however, spoke the mind of those rabbis who were not ready to give way to despair, nor to abandon themselves to a pietistic Christian form of mysticism as a response to the human predicament. In an address entitled "God and the World Crisis" in 1941, Rabbi Liebman said:

The present era with its new discoyeries of the typology of the human mind and the beginning of the cultivation of the continent of the subconsciousness, which has been throughout all these centuries an undiscovered jungle, contains, even though hidden from our immediate gaze, the seeds of a happier, more harmonious, better controlled and, therefore, more divine human society. It is in the slow imperceptible evolution of human genius that God's providence is imminent in our world.

Leibman characterized Niebuhr's assertion that "man is sinful at the very center of his personality" as a form of "intellectual masochism."

The Vision of God

Martin Marty, a perceptive Protestant critic has observed: "In a time when religion and national life are so fuzzily intermingled, the churches had better be ready to detail their vision of God, their hopes for man and their picture of the community."

Historian Daniel J. Boorstin suggests that in American culture an especially valuable role may be observed for those religions like Judaism, Catholicism, and the intransigent Protestant sects which remain in a sense "un-American" because they have not yet taken on the color of their environments. Such sects, while accepting the moral premises of their community, can still try to judge the community by some standard outside its own history. But even these religions often take on a peculiar American complexion and tend toward validating themselves by their accord with things as they are.

If it is asked in what ways Reform Jews have attempted to stand apart from the American experience and thereby to judge it on the basis of their own standards and history, then I think that we will have to conclude that the CCAR has been no trailblazer. Instead, it has contributed, in general, to the making of an American national secular religiosity that in many ways now competes with Reform Judaism for the souls of its constituents.

Rabbi Maurice Eisendrath, President of the U.A.H.C., in a Rosh Hashana confession has warned: The American Reform rabbi has been compelled "to acquire something of the Madison Avenue tint and the organization man touch;" . . . there are too many of us who are victims of "this creeping, even leaping indifferentism of our time; . . . no rebellion or discontinuity takes hold of our middle class Jews; . . . pastoral counseling rather than prophetic teaching is de rigueur now as rabbis succumb to the altogether unJewish distinctively Christian overemphasis on the salvation of the individual . . . rather than the galvanizing of the individual's resources for the redemption of society." The American synagogue is becoming "a blend of Jewish country club and Protestant church." We have permitted our lay leaders to assume their positions without meeting rigorous standards, and "we reward leadership on the basis of unJewish criteria, confusing business in the synagogue with the true business of Judaism."

Rabbi Charles Fleisher, at the turn of the century, declared: "We of America are 'a peculiar people' consecrated to that 'mission' of realizing democracy (which) is potentially a universal spiritual principle, aye a religion . . . Men like Washington, Samuel Adams, Jefferson, Lincoln (should be) placed literally in a calendar of saints to be reverenced by our future Americans as apostles of our republic." Unfortunately, what Rabbi Fleisher suggested be done has now been accomplished in America!

The question rabbinical leaders, therefore, must ask themselves is in what ways allegiance to the God of Abraham, Isaac, and Jacob ought now compel Jews to stand apart and in judgment of America's democratic society. And then we need consider the discipline by which to achieve such an effective apartness.

I am trying to say that we Jews first need to rediscover the particular God of the Hebraic experience. American impatience with matters theological must become particularly the burden of our educational effort. Otherwise how will we explain to our young why it should make a difference to them whether one works for racial integration as a youth member of Core, or for peace as a member of the Student Peace Union, or as a member of the National Federation of Temple Youth? What difference does it make in the quality of living if one is just a decent human being out of regard for good citizenship or if one is a decent human being out of regard for God's commandments?

Robin Williams, Jr. points out that "there is a marked tendency to regard religion as good in American society because it is useful in furthering other major values—in other words, to reverse the ends-means relation implied in the conception of religion as an ultimate value in experience."

How can we help our own Jews, let alone other Americans, understand that we serve God because that is man's profoundest expression of human freedom—rather than as a technique for securing socially sanctioned goals? Ought not Judaism confront Jews with a God who calls out to them for service and obedience, who responds not to men or ambition or pride but rather to the broken of heart and to the contrite of spirit? In their constant optimistic emphasis on man's capabilities and their insistent call upon him to engage in action—both characteristic of normative American values—do not American Jews often fail to recognize their relatedness to God in the brokenness of their spirit and in the inner quality of their spiritual life. The CCAR has only just begun to confront this continuing crisis in communicating a theology to the Jews.

The Pursuit of Social Justice

Where Jews have become deeply involved in the effort to achieve social justice, is it necessarily a reflection of their religious consciousness? Are they striving after God's Kingdom on earth, are they aware of responding to the Eternal's demand upon their behavior? Do they recognize that which is Jewish in their fulfillment of their American citizenship responsibilities? Nathan Glaser insists that "it is specious to say that American Jews express religious attitudes even indirectly in their concern for social problems. Whatever the origins of this concern, it is now divorced from religion. Its strength in the Jewish group has almost always come from nonreligious elements."

It is not the Jew's fault alone that this is the case in America. Again, as Robin Williams observes, "The (American) public generally assigns organized religion a special circumscribed place as the repository of values that are inherently of the highest good but that should be safely insulated and restricted to ceremonial occasions so that they cannot interfere too much with the ordinary business of the society."

If we Jews are serious about applying these insights of religion to the public order, then we had better give serious consideration to these three suggestions:

1. We ought increase the staff available to develop expertise on matters of social concern and provide a greater budget for the development of resources to educate our conscience.

2. Aware that the laity does not always follow the counsel of their religious leaders, we need increase the involvement of the laity in combined efforts at developing programs of social action.

3. At all times we ought define those religious insights and values that are particular to Judaism that compel our social action.

I am most distressed that we Jews consider resolution-making as an effective response to the demands of social change, and that we have permitted the language of law or secular political theory to substitute for religious concepts in undergirding our commitments to charity, justice, and peace.

The responsibility upon Judaism to be a prophetic faith derives not only from our own past religious tradition, but indeed it is the need of this moment in America, particularly at a time when the church and synagogue have voluntarily exiled themselves to suburbia.

Of new churches built between 1950 to 1960, 63½% of these were suburban, a National Council of Churches survey reveals; and the suburban trend in the Jewish community is even more marked.

Gibson Winter comments, "The captivity of the church is a national tragedy of the first order, for it occurs at a time when American position of world leadership requires a prophetic church at home. Suburban leadership is the antithesis of the prophetic note in the gospel."

Stanley Rowland explains, "When organized religion is completely accepted by the mass as no more than a pleasing and fashionable facet of culture, then it falls prey to the mass-produced platitude."

If Protestants have been particularly vocal in articulating their concern over the suburban captivity, the problem is no less severe for the Jew. We must confront again the living God who once called Moses into action from a burning bush not consumed. Then, like Moses, we must be willing to endure the dismay and distrust of our people as we demand of the Pharoahs of our own day "let my people go."

The Practice of Particularism

One of the consequences of World War II was that it brought to an end the ghettoization of Jew and Catholic. In the fire of the war Jews and Catholics earned for themselves an at homeness in America they had experienced only uneasily as long as they were considered alien or immigrant. Furthermore, the shift of political power from Protestant rural America to the urban centers populated with Catholics, Jews, and Negro minorities resulted in a reappraisal of status and rights. This confidence in American freedom, and the shift in political power has produced fresh Protestant-Catholic-Jewish conflicts: but as well, there is now a counter-reaction seeking to achieve harmony by emphasizing the responsibilities of each to the secular order.

Robin Williams observes that secularism is the inevitable consequence of pluralism. "A homogeneous society will be a sacred society marked by an absolute value system and intolerant of deviant behavior; whereas in a situation marked by contending groups, there are strong pressures toward secularization." Such secularization, after all, is required if we are to live together in one society. But it is also the enemy of particularism.

In our battle against sectarianism in the public school and against the establishment of Christian symbols as state-sanctioned forms for communicating civic virtues, the Jews have waged a noble battle; and this remains, in my view, the CCAR's outstanding contribution to America. In that battle we have called upon the church to recognize the integrity of its sancta and to question the propriety of their distorted misapplication in service of national and secular purposes. We have waged a battle for the preservation of the holy and the inviolability of conscience; but our posture has been that of a minority defending our own rights, securing our own status, and our victories have contributed inevitably to the growth of secularism. We are called upon, therefore, *now* to deal with the more difficult problem of the relation of religion to society in a pluralistic culture in such a way that we enhance religion without handicapping religions.

Now that devotional and liturgical rites may not be permitted in the public schools of the United States, the question still remains: what is the school's responsibility to the religious aspect of truth nurtured in Western civilization, and how can it fulfill that responsibility? There is no evidence that the CCAR has seriously put its mind to the resolution of this question. The role of religion in state-supported higher education, the place of information about religion where intrinsic to subject matter, the needs of children who attend state-licensed schools under church auspices, the possibilities of accommodation in working out shared time or released time arrangements, on all of these issues our response tends still to be formulaic instead of fresh and creative.

But the issue is larger than religion and public education. Beneath that there is the problem of religion in its particularity, and the relation of sectarianism to a secular culture. Nathan Glazer, for example, suggests that the growth of Jewish religious affiliation has nothing to do with religion. Rather, he says, "it is linked with the great movement to the suburbs and middle class values." These include such values as "respectability" and "the decline of all extremist movements whether left or right." Glazer is forcing us to ask ourselves whether our growth in religious membership is not, after all, an expression of nondenominational American secular religiosity rather than a specific commitment to a particularity of observances and belief? To be an American is to belong to some church, and it doesn't matter which church. Jews, traumatized by the shock of Hitler, made proud by the establishment of the State of Israel, join the synagogue today as a means of group identification, and in order to continue the existence of the Jewish people. But, as Glazer notes, "The ancient notion that Israel exists to serve the law is here reversed. It is argued that the law exists to serve Israel."

Rabbi Balfour Brickner asks: Is it desirable that we survive? And then he responds, in a recent essay in American Judaism by asserting: "If our survival is desirable it is because Judaism has a unique contribution to make to human existence." In order to strengthen the distinctive commitments, Brickner calls for "Jewish preparatory schools" under Reform auspices, and he argues the value of "voluntary Jewish enclaves."

These are controversial suggestions that reverse the whole course of Reform Judaism in America. Indeed, they are one answer to the problem of secularism and indifferentism. But are there not other more creative ways of relating religion to society so that all religions will be favored, none disadvantaged, and the freedom of conscience respected?

Even as we work at this problem in the decade to come, it is clear that Reform rabbis will wish to engage their faithful in the practice of their particularism, and in this effort we are no different than other confessional churches in today's America. But it suggests that tomorrow's America will be different.

"Indeed the idea that religion is handmaiden to democracy has made such headway," asserts Professor Arthur Mann, "that American Catholicism, American Protestantism, and American Judaism appear like parallel shoots on a common stock."

I suspect that once the blush of happiness at our religious concord is overcome, all of America's religious groups will want to reassert their sectarianism and to insist upon their unique integrity. The development of patterns of living together within the richness of our differences can become CCAR's contribution to a new America now aborning.

5

Legislation, Litigation, Dialogue— Methods Used to Achieve Religious Freedom in the United States

Foreword

AN EXAMINATION of American history reveals that social change in the relationship among America's religious groups has rarely been achieved without some degree of violence. Protestant dissenters, Roman Catholics, Jehovah Witnesses, Jews, each in turn have suffered physical assault because they challenged the prevailing conceptions of church-state relationship and insisted on a redefinition of religious freedom. Yet because of the unique structure of our democratic institutions, each change partakes of an *evolutionary* rather than a *revolutionary* character. Recourse has been available through the legislature and constitutional convention; and failing in that, minority groups have found the courts of the United States to be a bulwark of democracy, balancing political power so that justice might be pursued unfettered by mob passions or popular fashion. Finally, in this most recent period of American history, there has emerged the phenomenon of the dialogue between faith communities, suggesting to some the possibility that interreligious conflicts may also be resolved through understanding accommodations. It is instructive, therefore, to assess those methods by which the emerging pluralism of America has been confronted and the religious and civil rights of minority groups extended, mainly to consider that which in the past is still meaningful and how to handle contemporary interreligious conflicts as we shape the future.

In the earliest period of American history religious groups generally established on these shores the same patterns of church-state union that had prevailed in Europe. This earliest period is marked by widespread conflict and intolerance as each church used the powers of the state to enforce church law and to stifle dissent. Pluralism in creed or practice was considered scandalous.

With the adoption of the First Amendment to the Constitution of the United States a process was set in motion by which the church-state establishments within the states of the United States could be examined through legislative enactment and state constitutional convention. Provisions guaranteeing religious freedom were written into the law and a greater toleration for religious pluralism was evidenced. Nevertheless, since Protestants were such a predominant majority in the population, quasi-Protestant or Christian establishments still lingered within the law of the land.

The first most decisive challenge to the Protestant hegemony derived from the huge Catholic immigration to this country in the early and mid-1800's. Not everywhere were Catholics successful in their attack on the status quo arrangements, but frequently they were able to find state judiciaries more responsive to their need than the local or state legislature. By testing their rights through the courts Catholics stimulated the judiciary to a new recognition of its role in the shaping of the American democratic heritage.

It waited upon cases brought by the Jehovah Witnesses in the 1930's, however, before the Supreme Court of the United States assumed an active role, asserting its authority over infringements of religious liberty within the states of the United States. By virtue of this active role of the court—sharing in a sense the traditional functions of the legislature—Jews, members of the Ethical Culture Society, Unitarians, and atheists today have found decisive support in their contention that freedom *for* religion requires as well freedom *from* any form of state sanctioned or supported religion—even if it be of the nondenominational, non-Christian religion-in-general stripe.

Since World War II much of the fear and suspicion that blocked free communication among America's religious groups has been overcome and dialogue has emerged. At the very same moment members of the Supreme Court confess that there is "no single and clear measure by which precise application can readily and invariably demark the permissible from the impermissible" in defining that "wholesome neutrality" that is required of the state if religious freedom is to be maintained. Thus, there are religious and civic leaders who are hopeful now that the dialogue itself will produce such a degree of trust among America's religious communities that new patterns of relationship will develop without the tensions evoked either by utilization of political power or litigation.

What remains clear, of course, is that religious liberty is not a gift handed down from one generation to another. It has had to be achieved through conflict, and in every generation it has been redefined and stated anew. This chapter will attempt a brief review of that history with particular emphasis on the methods of achieving social change employed in each period.

The Period of Church-State Establishment

The earliest immigrants to America had themselves experienced intolerance in Europe. They sought the haven of these shores, therefore, in order to worship God without fear. But each group in turn used the powers of the magistrate to support its own dispensation. Dissenters had only the freedom to enter the wilderness and carve out their own enclave, as did Roger Williams. It was only at that point where the religious pluralism had become unmanageable and the violence perpetrated on dissenters had become so unconscionable that a few bold clergy and courageous legislators insisted on disestablishing the church and broadening the legislative provisions providing freedom of conscience.

Religion, indeed, was a prime motivating factor in immigration to this country and in the founding of the colonies but the earliest charters called for the establishment of the church and made no provision for disbelievers.

The grant to Sir Walter Raleigh, for example, contained an express proviso that laws of the new colony "should not be against the true Christian faith now professed in the Church of England." When in 1624 the charter of Virginia passed into the hands of the King, the Puritans were displaced and Anglican clergy alone were permitted to officiate in the colony. All believers and disbelievers alike were taxed to provide the Anglican clergy with "a fixed salary . . . a glebe house and land."

On their part the Puritans in Plymouth Colony and Massachusetts earned the rebuke of King Charles II for their cruel persecutions of the Anglicans; and when at last they relaxed their rigid church-state establishment they discriminated against Catholics, granting by charter in 1691 "liberty of conscience to all Christians except Papists." Until the revolutionary war nearly every American colony had strict laws outlawing "Papists." The law of the Province of New York in 1700 ordered perpetual imprisonment of Catholic priests performing religious rites or teaching Catholic doctrine. Maryland law in 1704 prohibited Catholic priests from baptizing children and in 1716 the state ordered severe punishment for public officials who attended Catholic Mass.

Even in those colonies where an effort was made to legislate some degree of toleration, the restrictions on religious freedom—if measured by contemporary American standards —would be considered abhorrent. In April 1649, for example, the Maryland Assembly under the regime of a Protestant governor, appointed by the Catholic Lord of Baltimore, passed a Toleration Act. It confessed that the enforcing of the conscience in matters of religion had frequently "fallen out to be of dangerous consequence." Nevertheless, it included penalties for the violation of the Sabbath. Those who denied the Holy Trinity or the Godhead of any of the Three Persons were to be punished with death and the confiscation of lands and goods.

Similarly, Roger Williams who had proclaimed that his

colony "might be for a shelter for persons distressed of conscience," offered no enthusiastic welcome to Quakers and overtly discouraged Catholics, although in this case, Jews were permitted to enter Rhode Island in large numbers.

William Penn's colony of Pennsylvania, by its Great Law of 1682, insured that no man could be molested or prejudiced for his or her conscientious persuasion or practice. In time, however, under pressure from England, first Catholics and then Jews were excluded from holding public office. A belief in "a future state of reward and punishment" was also required. An act passed in 1700 enjoined all citizens to attend church on Sunday or prove that they had been at home reading the Scriptures.

As late as the Revolutionary War, there were established churches in at least nine of the 13 original colonies and multiple establishments in four others.

Federal Disestablishment

The first most successful effort to disestablish the church from the state resulted from the Revolutionary War. In this case, not by evolution but rather by the fire of revolutionary passion America was set on its course of church-state separation.

Sentiment against the Church of England had inevitably accompanied the war against English political domination. Isaac Backus, aggressive leader of New England Baptists in that harsh period, for example, explained that Baptists joined the Revolutionary War because "the worst treatment received by Baptists came from the same principles and persons that the American war did . . . and finally because the deliverance of America might regain for Baptists their invaded rights." Hostility for the established English church was so marked that membership in the church dropped immediately and severely with the disestablishment after the War. It took 30 years for the church to regain any bit of its earlier prestige and standing in the community.

It was exactly such anger at the Anglican Church's use of coercion to compel fidelity to its creed and to obtain financial support for its clergy that stimulated the efforts of Thomas Jefferson and James Madison to enact a bill for religious freedom in Virginia; and its eventual adoption there paved the way for the Constitutional Amendment included in the Bill of Rights adopted in Philadelphia.

Virginia's Declaration of Rights of 1776 was the first legislative pronouncement that freedom of conscience was an inherent right of the individual. "Religion is the duty we owe to our Creator and the manner of discharging it can be directed only by reason and conviction, not by force and violence; and therefore all men are equally entitled to the free exercise of religion according to the dictates of their conscience . . ." The effort to have this Declaration condemn the existing Episcopal establishment, however, failed to muster enough votes and it took almost another ten years before the convictions of the pronouncement could be translated into law. The decisive turning point was reached in 1784-1785 when Patrick Henry introduced a bill containing a provision for support of teachers of the Christian religion. Designed to revive the tithes suspended for almost 12 years, the bill would have required all persons to contribute annually for the support of some Christian church or communion. Henry defended his proposal not as an aid to religion but as a service to the state. The preamble of the bill said "The general diffusion of Christian knowledge has a natural tendency to correct the morals of men, restrain their vices, and preserve the peace of the society . . ." It was expected that Protestant dissidents would support the bill, since they were also included in its benefits.

James Madison's "Remonstrance" effectively killed Patrick Henry's bill. "Who does not see," Madison asked, "that the same authority which can establish Christianity at the exclusion of all other religions, may establish with the same ease any particular sect of Christians in exclusion of all other sects?" Madison had no quarrel concerning the size of the proposed tax or that it would be given to all equally; rather the issue for him was the power of the state to impose *any* such tax for aid to religious education. "Religion is wholly exempt from it (the state's) cognizance," he asserted.

Similarly, Thomas Jefferson argued, ". . . even forcing him (a man) to support this or that teacher of his own religious persuasion, is depriving him of the comfortable liberty of giving his contributions to the particular pastors whose morals he would make his pattern . . ." Yet despite such arguments in favor of freedom from taxation for the support of religion, both Madison and Jefferson lent their weight to legislation that provided state sanction for religious morality in general. Madison and Jefferson supported a "Bill for Punishing Disturbers of Religious Worship and Sabbath Breakers." Jefferson's motion put teeth into a "Bill for Appointing Days of Public Fasting and Thanksgiving." Ministers who failed to preach a sermon suited to these state-appointed occasions could be fined, according to Jefferson's amendments, up to $50. Jefferson recommended nonsectarian instruction in the proof of God's existence within the system of higher public education.

The adoption of the Federal Constitution of 1789 and the Bill of Rights in 1791 stimulated a reconsideration within all the states of their obligations to protect freedom of religion for all men. The Constitution, however, restricted only the Federal Government from the establishment of religion. It had no binding power over the states; and although disestablishment had come quickly in the southernmost colonies under Anglican influence, the separation principle was only slowly achieved in the Congregational established states.

Massachusetts, for example, even in the midst of the Revolution of 1779, adopted a Constitution that provided that towns be required "to make suitable provision at their own expense for the public worship of God." Not until 1833 did Massachusetts complete its disestablishment.

In Connecticut, as late as 1816, the larger denominations sought support for a pluralistic establishment. They favored a bill for support of literature and religion. On a graduated scale, the bill provided sums for Yale, Episcopalians, Baptists, and Methodists. After a sharp two-year controversy, the measure was lost in the legislature by the small margin of ten votes out of 200 cast.

In 1784, New Hampshire adopted a provision in its Constitution which authorized "public support of Protestant teachers of piety, religion, and morality." The provision explained that "morality and piety rightly guaranteed on evangelical principles will give the best and greatest security to the government . . ." In 1792, New Hampshire's Constitutional Convention reaffirmed religious restrictions that had been written into the franchise. Baptists and Universalists were soon thereafter granted toleration but, as late as 1850, Catholic emancipation was overwhelmingly defeated. Even in 1868, this restriction was upheld by state court action. The dissenting judge insisted that "Practical construction shows that the Protestant test is anti-Catholic and nothing else." The word

"Protestant" was maintained in the New Hampshire Bill of Rights until 1902, when it was changed to "Christian." It provided: "Every denomination of Christian . . . shall be equally under the protection of the law although guaranteeing that no subordination of any one sect or denomination to another shall ever be established." In 1912, this symbolic Christian establishment was still retained by a votors' referendum in spite of strong denunciations of implied discrimination against Jews.

Although the Federal Government had no control over the establishment of religion in the original states, it did exercise its power when new states applied for membership in the Union. The Ordinances of 1787 passed by Congress for the government of the Northwest Territory guaranteed specifically that "No person deeming himself in a peaceable and orderly manner shall ever be molested on account of his mode of worship or religious sentiment . . ." It also provided that "Religion, morality, and knowledge being necessary to good government and the happiness of mankind, schools and the means of education shall forever be encouraged." It was presumed, evidently, that schools would teach morality based on generally accepted nonsectarian (Protestant) principles. Thus, while Congress prevented any establishment of religion in these new states, it nevertheless gave expression to an American policy of friendliness toward religion, acknowledging religion as a constructive ingredient in the shaping of public morality. Ohio, Indiana, Illinois, and Michigan were formed on this territory.

In 1798, Congress provided that the Southwest Territory also be administered under the same provisions. An issue arose over the situation in Texas. When Texas had belonged to Mexico, the Catholic Church was established by law and non-Catholics were restricted. The legislature of the new state, therefore, renegotiated the property rights of the Catholic Church and the Texas Declaration of Rights guaranteed religious freedom for all. Catholics sued in court to maintain state support of the clergy on the ground that the practice had been sanctioned by "previous system." The state court denied the claim, indicating that the Roman Catholic Church had "properly" been "reduced . . . from the high level of being the only national church to a level of equality with other denominations of religion." In light of this important change, added the court, "it could not for a moment be contended that assessments and contributions could be levied for the purpose of erecting church edifices and the support of ecclesiastics."

The constitutions of those states formed after the Civil War were required to provide an irrevocable ordinance that "Perfect toleration of religious sentiment shall be secured and no inhabitant of said state shall ever be molested in person or property on account of his or her mode of religious worship." The Compacts with Arizona, Idaho, Nevada, New Mexico, North Dakota, Utah, Washington, and Wyoming contain this provision. Colorado, Montana, and Oklahoma also accepted this ordinance in separate documents attached to their Constitutions.

The Federal influence assured an ever broader definition of the meaning of the separation between church and state and thus, as new states were added to the Union, the Constitutions were more restrictive in language than those of the original colonies. Utah alone, however, specified an absolute separation of church and state. Its Constitution of 1895 declared, "There shall be no union of church and state nor shall any church dominate the state or interfere with its functions." This forceful language reflected in part a reaction to the control Mormons had been exercising over the life of the territory.

During the Jackson Era, an unsuccessful effort was made in Congress to pass a tax in support of religion. After the Civil War, proposals were made to put the name of God in the Federal Constitution and to designate Christianity as the official religion of the country. Both of these proposals were turned aside and the new American experiment in church-state separation was affirmed as good for religion and society.

From 1776 to 1880, all states except two had adopted new Constitutions; all guaranteed religious liberty. Religious qualifications for holding public office however, were still retained. Arkansas, Maryland, Mississippi, North Carolina, Pennsylvania, South Carolina, Tennessee, and Texas disqualified an atheist. Pennsylvania and Tennessee required from their public officials a belief in the afterlife. The emerging public schools instituted devotional exercises of the Protestant liturgy and taught history from the perspective of New England Protestantism in an effort "to promote sound religion." In most states of the United States, Protestant conceptions of individual morality were, without question, established as the law of the land.

The first significant battles to enlarge the meaning of religious freedom and to guarantee the separation of church and state, therefore, as this review indicates, were fought out in the legislature and since the population of America was overwhelmingly Protestant, these were conflicts among Protestants. The Catholic and Jewish populations were minuscule and they were completely at the mercy and the good will of Protestant legislatures. Redress of injustice on appeal to the Supreme Court was impossible since the guarantees of religious liberty in the Federal Constitution were not yet applicable to the states.

On the other hand, Federal influence was felt as new states entered the Union and the pioneer territories provided haven for religious diversity. They were, by far, a more fertile soil for religious experimentalism. It is no accident that the Midwest became headquarters for German-speaking Reform Jews, Lutherans, and American-born Holiness and Pentecostal sects.

Religious Bigotry—A Hindrance to Religious Equality

The American Jewish historian, Rabbi Bertram Korn, points out that the struggle of the Jew for religious freedom in America was aided by well-motivated *individuals,* including Christians such as Roger Williams in Rhode Island and the Scotch Presbyterian, Thomas Kennedy, in Maryland. But it did not result from the opinion and action of *organized religious* bodies or of their official spokesmen. The general impulse to extend equal recognition to different creeds was the contribution of laymen who were frequently secularists, namely, those who were unaffiliated with religion or who were involved in positions of civil power where they acted in terms of their public responsibility rather than in accordance with the requirements of church dogma. Each advance in the area of religious freedom was actually made in a nonreligious context, through the courts or the legislature. *"Had there been no courts of law or legislatures or constitutional conventions,"* asserts Rabbi Korn, *"the ideal of religious liberty would not have been established as a realistic standard of behavior."*

Rabbi Korn recalls, for example, that when in 1858 for the first time Congress invited a rabbi to deliver the invocation, spokesmen for organized religion viewed the incident with horror. A Roman Catholic paper in Baltimore objected to any prayer in Congress which was not addressed to God through Jesus. A Baptist parson, William Brownlaw of Tennessee, denounced the legislators who had consented to this prayer by "a rabbi of the Hebrew denomination, the people who killed Christ." An Episcopal journal said ". . . it was with extreme sorrow and enormous disgust that we read the announcement . . . that Congressmen put forward as their official representative and mouthpiece before God . . . a minister who denies the Son of God. . . ."

In 1861, Congress passed a Volunteer Bill establishing that every chaplain must be "a regularly ordained minister of some Christian denomination. This was the first piece of legislature ever passed by Congress that discriminated against Jews. After a year of petitions, the law was changed. Many individual Christians supported President Lincoln in an effort to repair the injustice but no official organized Christian body raised its voice in support of the right of rabbis to serve as chaplains, although many official voices were raised in opposition. A YMCA meeting in Washington, called to consider the religious welfare of the Armed Forces, was quoted as insisting that even if Jewish soldiers were segregated into all-Jewish regiments, the leaders of the YMCA would still not be willing to approve the appointment of rabbis as chaplains. The periodical of the Cincinnati Presbyterian Church rejected the idea of Jewish chaplains with this strong editorial statement,

Our government has already gone at great length in this respect in appointing Roman Catholic and Universalist chaplains to the Army . . . these denominations at

least call themselves Christians and profess to honor the
law of Jesus, however much they really dishonor Him . . .
yet should this bill become a law, which God forbid
that it should, the government in effect says that one
might despise and reject the Savior of men and thus
trample underfoot the Son of God. . . .

Despite these occasional outbreaks of religious bigotry, the
significant point is that from the period of the adoption of the
Federal Constitution until the deluge of Catholic immigration, the legislative process itself was sufficient to extend religious freedom and to encompass within its concern the small
group of Jews, Catholics, and dissenters in America.

The situation changed remarkably with the Irish immigration. The good will of Protestant America was challenged by
a forthright claim on the part of the Catholics for a new
definition of religious liberty; and good will was found
wanting.

Catholics Exercise the Right to Litigate for Justice

Although it would be improper to suggest that the Catholics acted with a rationally designated strategy, a pattern of
action in the public order does emerge. At first, through reasonable requests to proper administrative channels, Catholics
sought redress for grievance. Failing in that, they attempted
legislative action and in one case organized politically for
such purposes. But still very much in the minority, Catholics
in general found themselves blocked and out-voted and so
they resorted at last to the use of the court. Violence and
harsh feeling accompanied their action at every step of the
way.

When the public schools of the United States were first instituted, Protestants generally insisted that their religious school systems be included within the public school funds and, in most cases, such requests were honored. The Common School Act of 1795, for example, provided funds for New York's denominational charity school. When in 1825, in New York City, the Public School Society refused to share its funds with church-related schools, the Protestants acquiesced but not the Catholic Church under Bishop Hughes. What rankled the mind of the Bishop was his conviction that the Public School Society itself was "a completely Protestant organization that taught Protestant Christianity." Its charter allowed it to teach in the schools "the sublime truth of religion and morality contained in Holy Scriptures."

In 1840, Bishop Hughes brought the conflict to a head by appearing on behalf of the Catholic schools before the Corporation of the city. He requested that the seven Catholic schools be permitted to share in the public school funds. The request was denied. Catholics thereupon took the case to the State Legislature, where the petition was again defeated although the lower house supported their demands. Reported nationally, this case fired the passions of the emerging Nativist movement. The Catholic victory in the lower statehouse of New York provided an ominous portent of the power of this "alien" and "foreign-dominated" church.

In bold reaction to the extremism of those Protestants who had organized an anti-Catholic political party in New York, a strictly Catholic ticket appeared for the first time. Its chief purpose was the attainment of public funds for the church schools. The anti-Catholic Know Nothing Party aligned with the Whigs suffered serious defeat at the polls and the Democrats, with Catholic support, were victorious. Catholics did not support their own Catholic party. The response to hatred was not, in the good judgment of most Catholics, political segregation. In January 1842, Governor Seward, redressing at least one injustice in the Protestant-Catholic relationship, signed a bill ending sectarian control of the Public School Society and he created a nonsectarian public school system.

If the Catholic Church could not obtain direct financial support for their church-related schools, they sought, at least, fringe benefits—aid for the secular education of inmates of Catholic orphanages, free textbooks, and bus transportation. This time, however, the Church pressed its claim through the courts. In 1848, the New York court ruled that an orphanage school under Catholic auspices was not "a common school" but in 1907, the court reversed itself. In 1922, a New York court ruled that furnishing textbooks was "an aid or a maintenance of a school of learning . . ." and therefore was prohibited by the State Constitution. Eventually, however, Catholics became strong enough in New York to achieve constitutional change. New York now provides free bus transportation for parochial school children, an exemption from the law prohibiting the use of public funds for sectarian purposes.

In general throughout the country during this period, Catholics found the judiciary more sensitive to their rights than the legislature and they made use of litigation increasingly as a means of achieving social change. The court, more than the legislature, was sheltered from the whirlwinds of prejudice then circulating the country. The court balanced the power of minorities and majorities; and justice was a determining factor rather than the cries of the mob.

The earliest cases challenging Protestant rituals and devotional exercises in the public schools of the United States were

brought by Catholic parents. As the Vicar General of the
Roman Catholic Diocese of New York explained in 1840:
The Holy Scriptures are read in the schools every day . . . The
Catholic Church tells her children that they must be taught
religion by authority . . . The Sects say: 'Read the bible; judge
for yourself . . .' The Protestant principle is therefore acted
upon, slyly inculcated, and the schools are sectarian."

It was not without suffering that the Catholics pressed their
claims. In Boston, 100 Catholic children were expelled from
the Elliott School for refusal to participate in Protestant religious exercises and one Catholic child was severely flogged.
In Philadelphia, riots erupted for three days over this issue,
leaving dead and wounded. In Maine, where the first Bible
reading case was argued in 1854, the Church school was
burned and the priests run out of town. The case was lost in
Maine and a similar case was lost in Massachusetts in 1859,
but Catholic litigants were successful in Ohio in 1872 and in
Wisconsin in 1890. The courts in Wisconsin rendered a decision the language of which foreshadowed the recent prayer
and Bible reading decisions of the Supreme Court.

Victories in the state courts of Louisiana and Mississippi
provided Catholic children with free textbooks, and then in
New Jersey with free bus transportation. The "child-benefit
theory" was clothed with the flesh of practicality. Catholics
now have a right to believe that their request for a share of the
public funds and services that are provided all school children
need not fall within Constitutional prohibition. Recognizing,
of course, that in some states the Constitution may be more
restrictive than the Federal Constitution, Catholics in recent
years have had to seek revision of State Constitutions. Such is
the case at present, for example, in Wisconsin where an effort
is now being made by Constitutional amendment to reverse a

1961 State Supreme Court decision providing that bus transportation to parochial school students violated the State Constitution.

The *Era of the Supreme Court*

The Jehovah Witnesses have been a minority group whose
small size precluded any expectations that by legislative action they could have achieved a consideration of their minority rights. Instead, they depended upon the courts to achieve
justice, creating for themselves a magnificent legal department. With the help of the American Civil Liberties Union,
the Jehovah Witnesses provided the Supreme Court opportunity to clarify in a substantial way the meaning of the First
Amendment. Like the Catholics before them, however, the
Jehovah Witnesses had to endure the hostility and outrages of
"patriotic" Americans.

Believing that God (Jehovah) alone is the proper object of
their devotion, the Jehovah Witnesses refuse to salute any
flag. During the 1930's, children of the Jehovah Witnesses
refused to engage in the flag salute exercises at the opening of
school day. Some 2,000 of them were summarily expelled
from public schools in 31 states. Local authorities in several
states attempted to brand the children "delinquent" by virtue
of their expulsion and to remove the children from their parents. More than 800 incidents of violence were perpetrated
against Witnesses and their churches. Known members of the
American Legion participated in 176 of these outrages.

Finally in 1943, the Supreme Court acknowledged that
patriotism could not be coerced and it excused those children
who, by sincere religious conviction, would not participate in
the flag salute exercises. In a stirring decision, Mr. Justice

Jackson pointed out that the flag salute exercise compelled students to declare a belief. "The flag salute is a form of utterance," he said. "Symbolism is a primitive but effective way of communicating ideas . . ." He added, "If there is any fixed star in our Constitutional constellation, it is that no official, high or petty, can prescribe what shall be orthodox in politics, nationalism, religion, or other matters of opinion or force citizens to confess by word or act their faith therein."

Despite the Court's decision, violence and expulsions continued. The Justice Department was compelled finally to circularize all United States attorneys, alerting them to their obligations to "uphold religious freedom as Constitutionally guaranteed."

A significant aspect of this case is that it marked a turning point in the Supreme Court's exercise of self-restraint where basic human liberties were involved. Earlier the Court had asserted that in a field

> where courts possess no marked and certainly no controlling competence . . . it is committed to the legislature as well as to the courts to guard cherished liberties and . . . it is constitutionally appropriate to fight out the wise use of legislative authority in the forum of public opinion and before legislative assemblies rather than to transfer such a contest to the judicial arena . . . where all the effective means of inducing political change are left free . . .

Now realizing, perhaps, that minorities cannot always overcome the hysteria of the moment and induce a reasoned consideration of their views, the Court asserted,

The very purpose of the Bill of Rights was to withdraw certain subjects from the vicissitudes of political controversy, to place them beyond the reach of minorities and officials, and to establish them as legal principles to be applied by the courts. One's right to life, liberty, and property, free speech, free press, freedom of worship and assembly, and other fundamental rights may not be submitted to vote, they depend on the outcome of no elections.

It is of interest to note at this point that Catholics sharply rebuked the Court for its earlier decision. Justice Frankfurter's reluctance to have the judiciary usurp the responsibility of legislature and his insistence that the people and the representatives themselves ought not rely on the Court "for the impossible task of assuring a vigorous, mature, self-respecting and tolerant democracy . . ." provoked a unanimous criticism from Catholic law journals. Representative of their viewpoint was the editorial of Reverend Paul L. Blakely in the Jesuit Magazine "America." Citing the valuable role of the Court in defending the right of Catholics to private schools as in the Oregon case, Blakely took off on Frankfurter's conclusion that "the courtroom is not the arena for debating issues of educational policy." "If that be true," queried Blakely, "where is our protection when the next campaign to close our schools through the Oregon method begins?"

In another case brought to the Court by the Jehovah Witnesses, the Court upheld the right of a religious group to distribute their literature and to seek converts even in spite of the "probability of excess and abuses." In this case, the Court, for the first time, clearly extended the protection of the 14th Amendment to the religious liberties protected by the First Amendment. It thereby gave itself jurisdiction over those actions of state authorities that, in its judgment, abridged religious freedom.

By these Jehovah Witness decisions, the Court catapulted itself into the center of the democratic process by which accommodations and adjustments are made among religious groups in our pluralistic society and by which the state regulates its relations to the church. The Court not only assumed a share with the legislature in developing patterns of church-state relationship, but it set itself up as the ultimate arbiter of conflicts among religious groups in this pluralistic society.

Jewish Community Benefited by Supreme Court

The Jewish community in the United States has been most benefited in recent years by the Court's active involvement in church-state issues. Jewish parents and Jewish agencies have been party to almost every First Amendment case that has made its way to the Supreme Court. The particular concern of Jews has been the place of religion in public education and the right of Sabbatarians to exemption from restrictive Sunday closing laws.

There was a time, however, when the Jews were too frightened to litigate. Anxiety over anti-Semitism inhibited the national public exposure consequent to the use of court action. Further, Jews were not yet certain that American jurists would appreciate their particular concerns. In former decisions, the Supreme Court, and to an ever greater degree State Courts, had included assertions that this was "a

Christian nation" or "a religious country." Jewish opposition to religious exercises in public schools and Christian symbols on public property could easily be misrepresented as an attack on religion and Christianity. Reform Jews, particularly, engaged in a major effort, ultilizing the methods of education and persuasion, to sensitize the conscience of Christian Americans but without any significant results. Despair over the ability of dialogue to achieve social change soon became evident.

Thus, when the Supreme Court demonstrated its new sensitivity for minority rights and extended its authority over infringements on religious liberty within the states, Jews were ready to make use of litigation.

Yet even at that point in American history in the 1940's, the institution of Court Suit still entailed some physical risk. The record indicates that Jewish parents who had protested Christian religious practices in the public schools endured cross burnings on their lawns, harassing telephone calls, the threat of economic boycott, and the mass distribution of anti-Semitic hate literature. But it must also be admitted that these acts of violence have been mild when compared to the past incidents in American history. Evidently Americans have reserved for interracial relations, the physical passion that once accompanied interreligious conflicts.

The *Educational Function of the Law*

The debate over the Court's decisions on prayer and Bible reading in the public schools and the testimony rendered at the Congressional hearings on a Constitutional amendment has provided an education for all American citizens on the meaning of religious freedom that the Jews never could have achieved by the publication of pamphlets or the organization of inter-clergy conversations.

This is not to deny that there is a widespread disobedience of the Court's decisions at the grass-roots level. Studies undertaken in cooperation with the NCCJ (National Conference of Christians and Jews), reveal that the majority of school systems, particularly in the rural parts of the United Sates, will continue with the regimen of religious practice, prayers, and Bible readings at the opening of their school day. But at the same time, educational and religious leaders have pointed to the crisis in morality occasioned by the fact that a public school will seek to instruct children in respect for the law and then break the law itself with an act of prayer.

Without doubt, we are entering a new period in the history of church-state relations in this country. As I have admitted, the Founding Fathers probably never intended by the First Amendment to exercise a federal control over state actions nor to remove from education its responsibility to communicate a religiously-sanctioned morality. While the instrumentalities of state and church were not to be intermingled, there was never any thought of creating barriers for the spiritual interpenetration of society. I have no doubt, however, that the Court acted properly when it considered state composed, sponsored, or sanctioned liturgy in the public school, whether voluntary or not, to be an establishment of religion. Indeed, the pluralism of our nation in this post-Protestant, even post-Christian, era required such a decision.

As Mr. Justice Brennan observed in the Schempp-Murray cases

> . . . our religious composition makes us a vastly more diverse people than were our forefathers. They knew

differences chiefly among Protestant sects. Today the nation is far more heterogeneous religiously, including as it does substantial minorities not only of Catholics and Jews, but as well those who worship according to no version of the Bible and those who worship no god at all . . . practices which may have been objectionable to no one in the time of Jefferson and Madison may today be highly offensive to many persons, the deeply devout and the nonbelievers alike.

Within the prayer decision the Court also recognized that it cannot separate religion from the state absolutely without itself becoming party to the establishment of a functional secularism as the philosophy that undergirds governmental action. The Court invoked a creative concept of "wholesome neutrality," recognizing thereby, that the law when rigidly separatist can be detrimental to religion. Some freedom must remain for cooperation between religion and state so that the secular purposes of the state may themselves be served, and the religious needs of the American people respected and accommodated. In the Schempps-Murray cases Justice Goldberg stated the issue well. He observed,

. . . untutored devotion to the concept of neutrality can lend to invocation or approval of results which partake not simply of the noninterference and noninvolvement with the religious which the Constitution commands, but of a brooding and pervasive devotion to the secular and a passive or even active hostility to the religious. Such results are not only not compelled by the Constitution but it seems to me are prohibited by it . . . government must inevitably take cognizance of the existence of religion and indeed, under certain circumstances, the First Amendment may require that it do so . . .

Apparently there is a vast political consensus that approves of such cooperation. Witness, for example, the lack of restriction against the use of public funds for secular instruction in church-related schools in the recent Congressionally-approved grants for higher education, The National Defense Education Act, and the Poverty Bill.

The fine line between wholesome and unwholesome neutrality, public service grants and aids to the church, teaching *about* religion as an aspect of secular education and the teaching *of* religion, remains hard to define. It is conceivable now that the Court will be confronted with a rash of lawsuits seeking adjudication of every fine point. There is now a danger that Americans will become litigious on the church-state issue.

In his review of the Supreme Court term of 1963, in the "Harvard Law Review," November 1964, Philip B. Kurland suggests that a consequence of the Court's work during this decade has been "the enhancement of judicial dominion at the expense of the power of other branches of government, national as well as state." Although acknowledging that the Court's thrust for equality is deserving of approbation, Professor Kurland suggests nevertheless, that "the most recent expansion of judicial authority has had a longer life than usual and shows no immediate likelihood of recession. At least there are no indications of self-restraint."

I, too, hope that the court will exercise self-discipline, realizing that there has been a benefit for democracy in our country that derives from the local control of public school policy.

Having set down broad principles, the Court ought not now seek to act as a national school board, but should rather allow the American people to work out some degree of consensus, if at all possible, through the process of dialogue.

The Emergence of Interreligious Dialogue

For the first time in American history, religious and community leaders are now talking to each other. We have reached such a point of maturity that each religious group has felt free to voice its opinion and seek justice for itself without fear of violent consequence and with some degree of assurance that views will be heard, understood, and reacted to civilly, whether in agreement or disagreement.

Under the auspices of the National Conference of Christians and Jews, dialogue groups of clergy now meet monthly in 55 cities of the United States to discuss issues of religious freedom; and with the cooperation of educational associations, national denominational bodies, and academic institutions, new approaches to the problems of religion in education and the financing of education are being explored.

Recourse to litigation alone as the ultimate arbiter of interreligious conflicts substitutes "constitutionally" for "righteousness" as the central political value. It diminishes the obligation of all to consider with each other that which is in the public good, and it delegates to the judiciary a responsibility that should also be shared by all citizens.

In recent years, Catholics particularly have been eager to seek political solutions to their requests for public funds for church-related school children, in contrast to adjudication. In the tension between the conflicting "good" of church-state separation and the excellence of the education of all America's school children, Catholics have wished to pin their hopes on the understanding and sympathy of the American people rather than on the Court. For the Court may have to choose from among these goods, whereas the American people, through the process of dialogue, may discover those programs that will somehow satisfactorily remain faithful to both concepts.

In a major address before an NCCJ sponsored institute on religion and law at the University of Chicago Law School, Senator Abraham Ribicoff supported such a viewpoint. He said,

> It is safe to predict that if the difficult cases in this field are one day decided by the Court it will either set aside much of the public support now going to private education, or more likely it will indicate a much wider area of permissiveness than is now in effect. This raises the question of do we really want a series of definitive answers from the Court on these most perplexing questions? Or more pointedly, do we want such answers now? Would it not be better to pursue the political process further to explore new approaches to the problem and try to develop a consensus within this country as to what should be done.

This review of history reveals that much of the conflict among American's religious communities resulted from the prejudice and the mistrust that existed between our faith communities. The emergence of the secular in education and a governmental policy of religious neutrality enable us to achieve public purpose without becoming entangled in religious wrangling. Is it not possible, therefore, to conceive that in an age of new trust, more will be allowable and less will have to be restricted? Cooperation between the church and state need not be seen as threatening if we trust the churches to be *servants of all mankind* rather than as the *executors of institutional investment*. Dialogue might help us to achieve not only a degree of trust but even an interreligious competition in sacrificial service, as against membership recruitment and church building.

Interreligious dialogue, however, is still in its beginning and it may be too soon to spin such dreams for it as a method of social change. Our democratic system properly still provides recourse to legislative enactment and to judicial review. All of these methods, however—legislation, litigation, and dialogue—have their strength and weakness. Of this we may be sure: we are living in a markedly new period of history in the relation of America's religious communities. It behooves us therefore to consider carefully how best we may witness to the vitality of the democratic process and demonstrate that love and service are still the true characteristics of religion.

6

The Education Act of 1965 and American Jewry

THE SMOKE has not yet cleared away, but the debris caused by the erruption over the church-state aspects of President Johnson's poverty and education measures is clearly visible. The united front usually maintained by the Jewish community on church-state issues is now torn asunder. The main line Protestant groups within the National Council of Churches gave their support to the President's proposals and left the Jewish "separationists" allied with only a small coalition of anti-Catholics, Protestant fundamentalists, P.O.A.U., Unitarians, and secularists. It used to be that Protestants overwhelmingly opposed any expenditure of public funds for church-related institutions—Jewish support of that position, therefore, was inconsequential—but now we are left exposed on the barricades. How did it happen and what are the issues?

Within the Jewish community the decisive consideration, clearly, was the precarious financial position of the all-day schools. They had failed to receive adequate Jewish communal support; and as the Orthodox leadership long had warned, they saw no alternative but to seek public funds. The number of Yeshivot has quadrupled in the last 15 years. There are now 303 Hebrew day schools in the United States in 95 communities, with a total enrollment of approximately 61,000 children. In 1964 only 31 communal Federation and Welfare Funds made grants to the all-day schools. Contributions ranged from $1,500 in Syracuse, New York to $116,000 in Chicago, Illinois. Federation appropriations totaled $595,631 against an estimated operating budget of $30,500,000. There is no questioning the fact, also, that the Orthodox Jewish community is least capable of supporting by itself such an educational undertaking. Torah u Mesorah officials report that an average tuition charge of $300 covers only 40% of the cost incurred.

Resistance to communal subvention of Orthodox parochial schools has been based in great measure on a principled opposition to a separatist ghettoized educational effort and as a reflection of the Jewish community's enthusiastic support of public education. Thus, at the 1961 General Assembly of the Conference of Jewish Federation and Welfare Funds, Amon Deinard explained that the Minneapolis Federation had turned down a request from the local day school because it was held "that an all-day Jewish school was a parochial school, and Jews, of all people, should oppose community financing of parochialism because it is destructive of the American concept of general public education . . . Jews should be in the forefront of the community in opposition to anything that would injure the spirit of free education."

Similar concerns motivated much of the organized Jewish community's opposition to the church-state aspects of the Education Bill. Leo Pfeffer in his testimony on behalf of the American Jewish Congress before the Senate Subcommittee on Education asserted, "Use of Federal Funds to finance parochial schools would . . . gravely endanger the continued existence of the public school system." Then, citing the experience of the Netherlands, he concluded, "The fragmentization of the public school system would be but one of the many unfortunate consequences of the initiation of a policy of dividing governmental education funds among religious groups. . . . The public schools . . . will become the stepchildren of tax raised funds, receiving only what is left after the sectarian forces have had their share." Rabbi Richard G. Hirsch in his testimony in behalf of the Commission on Social Action of Reform Judaism asserted:

. . . We are firmly committed to our public school system as the bulwark for preserving America's democratic heritage and advancing its civilization . . . By tending to equate public and church schools in the eyes of the law as equally entitled to public support this bill will greatly stimulate the creation of separate parochial school systems in every denomination . . . As a network of parochial schools mushrooms, support for public schools would constantly be diluted.

He too, cited the situation in Holland as case in point.

It might be of interest here to note that the use of the situation in Holland as a portent of what might happen in America, should public funds be made available to church-related schools, has been rejected by leading scholars of comparative education. Recently at a conference on Religion, Education, and the Law, Dr. Theodore L. Reller, Dean of the University of the California School of Education, reviewed the relationship between public and church-related schools in Canada, England, and the Netherlands. Dr. Reller observed that none of these educational experiments had produced a "model" solution for the Federal Aid in question in the United States. In the Netherlands, he pointed out, subsidies to church-related schools brought "relative peace" to warring factions that already had compartmentalized and divided Dutch social, cultural, and economic life. The school arrangement, therefore, mirrored the existence of a system "dikes in the mental life of the Dutch," a situation completely dissimilar to that which prevails here. Concluding his paper, Dr. Reller confessed,

I undertook this review of practices in the hope that I might find a model or models of practice which might be recommended to Americans for serious consideration. I have not found such models. The historical background of this problem in the countries considered is very different from the background in the United States. All three of these societies are composed of far less religiously diverse and heterogeneous people than the United States. The existing governmental situations, constitutions, and statutes are different. The traditions of the societies, especially in regard to the relations of church and state are markedly different . . . Each nation will have to work through this problem in its own fashion for its own time, and there is no one solution.

While major Jewish organizational leadership articulated their fear that support of church-related schools would weaken public education, an opposite point of view was maintained by Rabbi Maurice Sherer, Executive Vice President of the Agudath Israel of America. He testified that it was never American policy to favor a public school system over others, that parochial schools contributed to the enrichment of American democracy and that America itself would be injured were excellence in education not maintained in all schools. Excellence required public subvention for impoverished private school children. He said:

Our Founding Fathers never intended our children to be raised in a monolithic educational straitjacket . . . Our educational plan is a mosaic, with the freeplay of the many faceted cultures of our people blooming into the molding of an informed, dedicated, and loyal citizenry . . . To compel our children because of the staggering financial hardships suffered by their schools to study in overcrowded classrooms and in makeshift annexes, as is the norm in so many communities, is more than an injust obstruction to their educational progress —it actually weakens the very structure of the entire American educational efforts.

Orthodox leaders added that whether private schools enriched American education or not, Jews ought be motivated by such a strong commitment to the strengthening of Jewish education that they would be willing to accept money from any source, including the government. This was the position of the Lubovitcher Rebbe Menachen Shneerson. He joined to his philosophic arguments the political stricture that only Orthodox Jews, at any rate, were qualified to make judgments on such issues. He said:

> One of the greatest frailties in contemporary Jewish life is the complacency toward the Torah—true education of our youth. In our generation we have become the unfortunate witnesses of the tragic fruits of this complacency—intermarriage and assimilation. Parents who neglected the Torah education of their children, thinking that matters would somehow take their proper course without it, or that it just wasn't that important—without realizing the consequences—have become victims of devastated homes and disgraced families because of their children's behavior.
>
> Elements foreign to the Torah way of life beckon the Jew to come and share their society, but the Jew can never acquiesce to this society for a Jew cannot survive in a world devoid of Torah, just as fish cannot live without water.
>
> Jewish education and the training of youth are the most cardinal precepts of the Jewish faith. Therefore, the entire matter of Federal Aid to parochial schools, so far as Jews are concerned, should rest in the hands of the Hallachikly, competent Jewish clergy, and certainly not in the hands of Jewish laymen or organizations.

Orthodox leadership chose to ignore that Reform and Conservative clergy had expressed alarm at the child-benefit formula. The American Jewish Congress was used exclusively as their foil. Thus, they tried to create in the public mind a distinction between a "religious" position and a "secular" one (this is a ploy that Reform Jews also tend to use when it suits their purposes). When Rabbi Amos Bunin, Chairman of the Executive Committee of the National Society for Hebrew Day Schools, appeared at the Senate hearings, Senator Randolph of West Virginia asked him how he could account for the fact that the American Jewish Congress opposed the bill. Rabbi Bunin answered, "The American Jewish Congress does not represent the religious community. It ill behooves this organization to try to protect the religious freedom of the Jewish community or, for that matter, of other faith groups, when that religious leadership endorses the bill and sees in it no threat whatsoever to religious freedom and, on the contrary, expects the strengthening of religious freedom to emerge from the enactment of the bill."

If Rabbi Bunin, on his part, had no right to speak for all of religious Jewry, it was clear nevertheless, that the predominant majority of Protestant denominations did favor the measure, as did the educational establishment, including the National Educational Association and the American Federation of Teachers of the AFL-CIO. These groups seemed convinced that this was the year that a Federal Aid to Education measure had to be adopted, even if some of the money were to be "drained off" to the private schools. The hard fact was that local and state revenues were and are inadequate to do the job of financing education. The cost of public education has been shared in the following ways: 56.7% from local sources, 39% from state governments, and 4.3% from the Federal Government. In 1962-1963 expenditures for per pupil education revealed a spread from a high of $645 to a low of $230. Estimating, then, that the cost of education will double in the next decade, and noting that there is a gross inequality in education at present, and that the only substantial resource of funds lies within the treasury of the Federal Government, the Rockefeller Report on Education concluded, "It will not be enough to meet the problem grudgingly or with a little more money. The nation's need for education is immediate; and education is expensive."

It should also be added that not everyone believed that monies expended to aid impoverished or handicapped children in church-related schools was a "drain." For many, the more important issue was that education for all children be improved! It was exactly this emphasis on 1) the use of public money chiefly and substantially in assistance of the poverty-stricken and 2) the devising of a formula to provide these monies for the benefit of children rather than school systems, that tipped the scale. Dr. Arthur S. Fleming, former Secretary of the United States Department of Health, Education, and Welfare, and presently President of Oregon State University, testifying in behalf of the National Council of Churches, explained, ". . . The Board [of the National Council of Churches] joined those who, in confronting the church and state issue, have drawn a line between assistance to students in private schools and assistance to private schools." R. H. Edwin Espy, General Secretary of the National Council of Churches was later to wire Senator Wayne Morse, "The General Board of the NCC . . . is willing that children attending nonpublic schools share in that aid through publicly administered arrangements such as dual enrollment."

Rabbi Sherer, in his testimony, similarly made it clear that Orthodox Jews were seeking no "government assistance for the religious studies program of Jewish all-day schools." He said that Jewish parents, "shouldered this heavy obligation willingly and in good grace." They seek government support for "general studies programs of the schools which meet all of the requirements of each state . . . Why should these parents be penalized with the heavy yoke of double taxation as they struggle to meet the skyrocketing costs of independently maintaining dual programs?"

It was exactly to this issue that Rabbi Richard Hirsch directed his testimony.

We deceive ourselves and the nation, if we use semantics to conceal what has actually occurred. Merely to insert language directing that tax monies be "for the use of children and teachers" rather than for schools, does not change the essential character of the recipient or the use to which the money is put. Everything connected with any educational system is "for the use of children and teachers."

Despite Rabbi Hirsch's eloquence, the fact is that there are constitutional precedents that have been upheld in several decisions of the Supreme Court, which have affirmed that the First Amendment is not violated when public services such as bus transportation or textbooks are provided to all school children without discrimination. While such child benefits may indirectly benefit a church-related school, the Supreme Court has not yet prohibited such benefits; nor is it certain that they will so rule.

Nevertheless, the National Council of Churches pressed for safeguards. These included:

1) That benefits intended for all children be determined and administered directly by public agencies.

2) That religious institutions be prohibited from acquiring property or the services of personnel thereby.

3) That such benefits not be used directly or indirectly for

the inculcation of religion or the teaching of sectarian doctrines.

4) That there be no discrimination by race, religion, class, or national origin in the distribution of such benefits.

The language in the bill was changed appropriately. In this spirit, the Office of Education has now concluded nine regional conferences where it sought from all concerned organizations additional proposals for safeguards to be written into the administrative regulations.

Jewish agencies, however, refused to be mollified. The day after the bill's passage, the American Jewish Congress announced that it would institute a lawsuit. The NCRAC proposed safeguards that are restrictive in the extreme. For example, NCRAC proposes that private or church-owned premises shall be used to supply educational services only if "it is impossible to use publicly owned premises." The Act itself specifically provides that the local public agency may not offer services or programs that will inure to the enrichment of any private institution. Similarly, it withholds funds for the payment of private school teachers, nor is the program intended to finance any construction or purchase of equipment that will be to the financial advantage of the nonpublic institutions. Nevertheless, the bill provides some leeway for public authority, in cooperation and in consultation with private school administrators, to make arrangements as to the location and the nature of the educational programs best suited to the needs of the total community.

It appears that it is exactly this requirement for such consultation that disturbs the Jewish agencies. Rabbi Hirsch testified: "It has been most disturbing to hear proponents of this bill in its present form, speak of the great 'partnerships' that it fosters between public and private schools. Public and sectarian schools can no more be considered partners than can church and state be partners."

In contrast to the harshness of these words, the National Council of Churches, even before the shared-time concept of supplementary educational facilities had been written into the Education Act, expressed its sensitivity to the financial burden of the parents of parochial school children; it welcomed, therefore, cooperation between public and parochial school administrators in an effort to deal with this problem. In an official statement issued June 4, 1964, the General Board of the NCC wrote: "Protestants and Orthodox are conscious of the financial difficulties under which their own and Catholic brethren and others labor in supporting two systems. While this predicament is not accurately described as 'double taxation,' it does involve additional cost. We are concerned as Christians to explore dual school enrollments as one possible solution to this problem."

An atmosphere of tension towards this proposal has been generated within the Jewish community. The Central Conference of American Rabbis, for example, repeated, in both 1963 and 1964, the warning that shared-time may "accentuate religious differences; it may involve religious functionaries in various aspects of public school administration, curriculum planning, and scheduling; it may result in derogating from the importance of the public school by assigning to it less important subjects while imposing upon it greater administrative burdens; and it may encourage proliferation of sectarian schools producing many separate school systems."

In contrast, Dr. C. Emanuel Carlson, Executive Director of the Baptist Joint Committee on Public Affairs and a staunch separationist, has suggested that the dual enrollment provision of the Education Act might strengthen rather than weaken public education.

It is difficult to see how an aggressive expansion and improvement of public education can fail to reduce the proportionate contribution of church schools. Dual enrollment can even be a precursor to a major transfer of pupils from private to public schools . . . The introduction of some public instruction into the parochial school pupil's program both by special services and by publicly selected instructional materials, seems likely to reduce the sectarianism of the private school pupil's experiences. Some democratic and general contacts and appreciation would normally result.

It would appear that the glass is half full or half empty, depending upon who is the observer. Of greater factual relevance are the findings issued by the Office of Education as a result of its comprehensive evaluation of shared-time programs currently in existence. The Office of Education sent a team of four specialists, two in law and two in elementary and secondary education, to make an in-depth study of how students, public and private school administrators, and parents felt about the program in nine different cities.

Almost all of the public school officials agreed that dual enrollment had extended the benefits of public school courses, special equipment and special speech and reading classes to pupils who otherwise would not have had them. They felt also that dually enrolled students had more opportunity to become acquainted with the diverse viewpoints in the community. All in all, the public school people said the program was a powerful instrument for unity; as a result of it, the Catholic community had greater understanding of the public schools and was more inclined to support public school issues at the polls.

Of interest also because it bears out Dr. Carlson's expectations rather than the fears of the CCAR, the report revealed that nonpublic school officials saw some "disadvantages." They saw that "some of the dually enrolled students lost their parochial school identity. They wondered whether dually enrolled students might not be inclined to transfer to public schools as full-time students."

Thus, Catholic administrators revealed their fears that the new educational program might weaken their parochial school system even as Jewish leaders seemed concerned that the program will weaken the public school system. In my estimation, both are wrong. As I see the situation, it appears that the unfreezing of Federal Funds will now enable public education to attain to the excellence America deserves. American public schools will be strengthened by this Education Act, not weakened by it. At the same time, approximately half the Catholics and a lesser percentage of Jews and Protestants will take advantage of the minimal funds available to strengthen sectarian education. But, emerging out of the use of shared facilities and the cooperative relationship between public and private school administrators, I see not a fragmentation of education but rather, a new experience of unity-within-diversity in America. We shall see ourselves not as institutionalized antagonists barricaded behind stone buildings, but rather we shall recognize the needs of all children to achieve their highest capacity. Cooperating together in the pursuit of excellence, we shall strengthen our unity and be enriched by our differences.

The present educational program makes it a matter of public responsibility to help all children achieve the best education of which America is capable, regardless of their differences in religion or race or the school system they attend. It may well be that as this program matures, the trust it engenders will prepare us for an even more profound pattern of interreligious relations and church-state cooperation.

The problems of our time require both that religious groups pull together, and that the Federal Government involve itself in more areas of human life. In my estimation Rabbi Hirsch was wrong when he asserted that church and state could never be "partners." They are already in a close cooperative relationship. This was inevitable. If the government is not to destroy completely private agencies and institutional freedom, then it must find ways of accommodating to, using the services of, and cooperating with religion; just as religion will have a stake in seeking to mold, shape, inform, influence, and cooperate with the government as it performs essential public services which overlap the moral concerns of religion. It is not surprising then to realize, as the Baptist Joint Committee has recently disclosed, that church agencies are now eligible for funds from more than 115 governmental programs. Billions of dollars are now being expended by the government for scientific research, the creation of public health facilities, old age programs, youth rehabilitation, and in the war against poverty. In many communities Jewish Federation agencies now report that almost half their operating funds come from governmental sources as against Community Chest or Jewish Federation subvention, and the percentage of governmental funds is increasing rapidly.

Thirty-three Jewish supported hospitals reported that the tax funds they received between 1958-1963 increased 13 million as against an increase of only seven million from Federation funds. Forty-nine percent of the receipts of 68 Jewish Family and Child Care agencies was provided by tax funds. 5.6 million of tax funds were given to 57 Jewish Old Age Homes as against 3.7 million given by Community Chests and Jewish Federations.

In the field of education the G. I. Bill of Rights, the availability of NDEA money, the Higher Education Facilities Act as well as the newly enacted Poverty Education Acts, suggest that there is certainly a partnership, or at least a cooperative relationship, in the making between big government and the church-related educational institutions.

Can we reverse this trend? I think not. I do agree that we must remain vigilant so that the tax funds are not misused or misappropriated and that direct grants are not given in support of specific religious programming. The present laws adequately seem to assure a formal separation between church and state. For those who are dissatisfied with this arrangement, however, and who dissent from this emerging pattern of cooperation, the Supreme Court will be available for final adjudication. It is important that Americans protect the right of this minority who will wish to engage in litigation. But I must admit that my own personal sympathies on this issue are with the Johnson consensus.

7

Religious Pluralism—A Jewish View

JEWS BELIEVE that we live in an unredeemed world. It is this stiff-necked assertion that distinguishes the Jew in a most relevant way from the Christian. For, in his denial that the Christ has come, the Jew makes judgment that the world still reflects something of the "void and formlessness" of its origin and is in an unfinished state; and that man need still struggle to bring a harmony, a purposefulness, a wholeness to the competing, conflicting instincts of his fleshly inheritance. In our judgment, all the evidence of reality testifies that redemption has not yet made its presence felt. It is afar off. "In *that* day the Lord shall be one and his name one."

I

What other people in all of history have suffered so cruelly the cold cut of the Crusader's sword, the flaming destructiveness of the Inquisitor's stake, the bestial perversion of man's genius evident in the efficient transportation of millions to scientifically-arranged experiments in barbarism? Of our flesh and bones, not too long ago, fellow human beings fashioned soap and lampshades.

One of the questions that pervaded all of the testimony at the Eichmann trial was the haunting query of Jewish youth to their elders, "Why did you let them take you away so easily? Why didn't you die fighting?" And the paradoxical answer was that, despite an awareness of the unredeemed nature of man, Jews could not believe their neighbors to be so ruthlessly inhuman. Even when escapees warned that the trucks and trains transported the Jews to tragedy and not to the slave labor camps, the victims refused to believe that man could really perpetrate such cruelty upon another in such mass, brutal, and gross form. This assertion that Jews believe the world yet unredeemed and that the Messiah whose presence provides assurance of redemption has not yet come, is, therefore, a statement of profound significance. It bespeaks a momentous difference between Jew and Christian and marks out the first distinguishing characteristic that must be noted if the social behavior of the Jew is to be comprehended. Where the Christian can believe that faith saves, the Jew can hold to no such simple prescription for the world's ills. Rather its complex, complicated nature must be worked at constantly and a variety of antidotes employed, experimented with, and sought after. There is a frantic quality in the Jew's pursuit after social change.

This leads to the second characteristic of the Jew's involvement in the social order. That is, the Jew must constantly battle the fatigue, the discouragement, the despair that inevitably accompany an awareness that man and his world are unredeemed. The consolation of the Jew, if it is that at all, is the fantastic notion that God, who commenced the creation, calls upon man now to assist in its completion. And the Jew accepts the unredeemed world as a challenge. Salvation is to be sought in the good work of reshaping the world. Man is commanded to work at it, to try to make it whole, to provide a purpose and a meaning to life, to lift up all his being, his work, his striving, his creation, his gifts before the Lord in a service of love toward other men. This is all man is called upon to do; it is quite enough. God in his own time will send the Messiah and will justify all sacrifice and all martyrdom. God in his own time will right the wrongs and restore the balance. This confidence reconciles; it enables man to know that although it is not his right to desist from the work, he need not finish it. He serves mankind and the Lord, too, by striving for justice and pursuing peace, by engaging in works of charity and fashioning things of use and beauty. Man knows well that all his efforts and all his creations are deficient by virtue of his human frailty and creaturely limitations. Nevertheless, for such purpose was man fashioned in the image of God; and the Holy One, blessed be he, will in his own time proclaim an "end of days" after his own fashion.

This is not to say that the faith of the Jew is not often shaken by the condition of God's world and the continual backsliding of God's favorite creation, man. The rabbis of old who taught theology through parables relate:

A man was wandering from place to place and saw a castle on fire. He said "It seems this castle is without a master." Then the master of the castle looked at him and said "I am the master of the castle." So when Abraham said "It seems the world is without a master," the Holy One, blessed be he, looked out at him and said to him, "I am the master of the world."

Thus the rabbis asserted God's sovereignty over the universe, that is, over a castle on fire; acknowledging, however, that man shared a responsibility for keeping it in order, and perhaps for having set the castle on fire. It seems, at any rate, that God does not will to run the castle alone.

Thus in another parable it is related:

> In the hour when the Holy One, blessed be he, created the first man, he took him and let him pass before all the trees in the Garden of Eden and said to him, "See my works, how fine and excellent they are. All that I have created, for you have I created it. Think upon this and do not corrupt and desolate my world. For if you corrupt it, there is no one to set it right after you."

The crucial role of man in completing God's creation, and in caring for his universe is asserted over and over. As an aside, we should note that the confidence of the rabbis in man's achievements and abilities was not so simple. It is related:

> For two years and a half there was a difference between the school of Shammai and the school of Hillel. The one school said it were better for man *not* to have been created; and the other school said it were better for man to have been created. They voted and concluded it were better for man *not* to have been created; but now that he has been, let him search his deeds.

Emphasis was placed, as you see, upon the importance of the work of man, even as man's limitations were tragically noted.

By what standard shall man measure his work and evaluate it? Toward what purpose shall he search his deeds? The rabbis instructed that man's labor must be in harmony with the inherent nature of God's purpose. That is, as the rabbis taught, "The world stands upon the pillar of the Righteous." It is alone and only because of the good works of man in this world that God permits the universe to endure. Rabbi Yose used to say, "Woe to the creatures that see and know not what they see, stand and know not upon what they stand." "Upon what does the earth stand?" the students asked. The rabbis, in reply, attempted to delineate those values and ideals around which life must be organized and upon which the universe must rest. Finally narrowing their list down to one, in which all other virtues are included, Rabbi Eleazar ben Shammai taught, "[The world stands] upon one pillar and its name is the Righteous; for it is said in Proverbs 10:25, 'But the Righteous are the foundation of the world.' "

Indeed, added the rabbis, it is through works of righteousness that man catches a glimpse of his Maker.

"How does a man find his Father, who is in heaven?" asked a student. The rabbi replied, "He finds him by good deeds and the study of the Torah. And the Holy One, blessed be he," added the rabbi, "finds man through love, through brotherhood, through respect, through companionship, through truth, through peace, through humility, through studious session, through service of the masters, through the discussion of students, through a good heart, through decency, through No that is really No, through Yes that is really Yes."

The Jew is commanded, therefore, to influence the public order and to shape society, to work for justice and to establish righteousness, as a divine commission. Whether there be heaven or no, hope for life eternal, reward or punishment, the point is that the Jew must involve himself in the concerns of the world, because to do otherwise is disobedience; because it is in service to other men that man may look upon the face of God. God seeks for man in man's righteous and charitable relations with other men. There is no relation to God that does not include as well the other man.

II

This leads us to another dimension in the Jewish conception of man's responsibility for the public order—the unique role of the collective fellowship, that is, the distinct role of the people of Israel. It is in the covenanted relation to a chosen people that God works out his purpose in history; and it is by the corporate witness of people in society, sharing the duties and responsibilities of their collectivity, that man will and can fulfill God's hopes for man. So the holy society viewed those laws that govern the equitable distribution of the earth's produce and provided for just relationships between employer and laborer, merchant, tradesman and consumer, the judge and the litigants, father and son, husband and wife, neighbor and neighbor—as religious law. Such law was as compelling and binding, even more so, than laws governing the cultistic requirements of ritual service to the divinity. "I despise your feasts and your burnt offerings," shouts the Prophet. Religiosity without religion, prayer without good works, ritual without neighborliness, is an abhorrence to the Lord. To this very day, in the contemporary Jewish view, the striving for a desegregated society, for a world well-fed, well-clothed, well-housed, for a world at peace is considered as an act of worship. There is no social or political issue of any significance that does not presume a moral position. Therefore, there is not, nor can there be, any separation between politics and religion.

God's demand of us that we seek justice involves us in shaping laws and influencing legislation. For justice is not real unless it is corporate in nature; there must be one law for all men. There must be corporate remedies for corporate ailments. There must be a joining together of resources to achieve a society wherein justice may prevail. In this view, therefore, the state in its essence is not a principality antagonistic to the church.[1] It is rather one of the domains in which the synagogue seeks to give concrete expression to the values nourished and cherished in the faith. The state is the God-appointed vehicle through which men achieve their public and common good. The Jews are not anarchists; they do not look for a "withering away" of the state. This explains why the Jews in America generally have supported all measures to use the resources of the state in order to achieve public good—a view that has frequently conflicted with a traditional Protestant morality of individualism and distrust of the state.

The traditional Jewish view corresponds more closely to the theology of the established churches and the traditional teachings of Roman Catholicism. In this traditional Jewish view, there is no separation between religion and state, nor between synagogue and state, for they mutually serve, each in fulfillment of God's purpose for man. The Judaism that proclaims belief in the universal brotherhood of man and strives for a world governed by one international law of righteousness also paradoxically maintains the importance of the par-

---

[1] Church is used here and throughout, unless specifically noted, in a generic sense. It includes synagogue and church. Where "synagogue" is used I refer specifically to Jewish viewpoints.

ticularity of each people and their state—for the holy people, by their laws establishing a just society, give witness to God's hand in history and his living presence in their midst. Zionism is not a secular movement in Judaism; it has a profound religious significance and dimension.

This, then, is a traditional view of Judaism: Man is called upon by God to do justly and to love mercy. He must consider himself interrelated to and responsible for the destiny of his brother. Using the law and powers of the state, he reaches toward a realization of God's kingdom on earth, which, through its corporate quality, serves the individual need. But man is frail and sinful, a backslider and unredeemed; better that he were not created nor burdened by this awful responsibility—but he is. Doing God's will is not easy. It challenges a man's faith and overwhelms his spirit. Nevertheless, God assures man that such service of him is perfect freedom; and in the end of time, when the Messiah has come, there will be understanding and quietness forever.

III

Obviously this theological prologue does not take account of the fact of religious pluralism. But how can theology take account of pluralism? Theology deals with one witness, with the witness and the responsibilities of one people in covenanted relationship to their Lord. It does not deal with the witness of two or three peoples; it does not deal with the problems attendant to a society where conflicting witnesses contend with each other to legislate morality, each declaring it speaks in the name of God.

I am aware, therefore, that in this cursory examination of the theological justification for the synagogue's involvement in and concern for the social order I have stimulated many more questions than I have answered. For the thesis thus far presented presumes a monolithic society where most men will share the same basic religious convictions. Nor does this theological view take into account the known tendency of the church itself to perpetrate evil when given undue access to the power of the state; nor the history of the state's persecution and perversion of the church and the individual.

It is, in fact, these very historic factors that have influenced many rabbis to abandon traditional Jewish theology when discussing church-state relations, and instead defensively to invoke those secular constitutional and historic arrangements that might provide them some safeguard against Christian imposition. Gratefully Jews have invoked the Protestant tradition of church-state separation in this country, even while rejecting other traditional Protestant conceptions that accompanied this particular free Protestant church defense against the established church.

Thus, the paradoxical phenomenon—the Jews support a secular state and lift up the religious liberty of the individual as central in America. Whereas, in Israel, where the Jews are a majority, the state officially supports and aids all religions and defends particularly the freedom of the religious community against the demands of the individual who wishes to be free of any religion. In Israel, on the one hand, the Christian, Moslem, and Jew can observe his own Sabbath without any disability—a situation that does not prevail in enlightened America. On the other hand, in Israel, you must be a member of a religious community. There is no possibility of marriage, divorce, or burial outside of religious jurisdiction.

I ought to make it very clear that American Jews who are mindful of the contradiction between their American position and the situation in Israel, have consistently urged that church and state be separated in the Holy Land as well. Jews are not involved here in a manipulative situation where they are suggesting in one situation where they are a minority one set of arrangements, and in another situation where they are the majority another set of arrangements. This relation between the practice of the Jew in Israel and the position he maintains in America nevertheless points to a tension within which the traditional theology finds itself. That is, a conviction on the one hand that the state and the synagogue must together declare their existence under God and each in their own fashion serve the purpose of fulfilling his will, and the requirement in a pluralistic society on the other hand that the state may not provide advantage for one religious group as against another, nor compel religious belief or practice, nor serve the narrow sectarian purposes of any one religion or all religions, recognizing the existence of individuals who hold to no belief; in a word, the state must remain secular.

I presume I do not need to rehearse the impositions upon the Jews throughout Western civilization that have led them to shudder today at the suggestion that there ought to be an interrelatedness between religion and government and church and state. Even in America the Jew today suffers unconscionable intrusions upon his religious liberty. His children were compelled to invoke the Trinity in public school prayer ceremonies each morning; and to declare the heretical belief that the Christ is born each Christmas during the public school carol sing. Or if a Bible class is conducted on school property, as it is in several of the states, the Jewish child in some communities may have the option of either sitting in the cloakroom or in the principal's office, neither so very desirable. If the Jew observes the Sabbath on the seventh day, the day which God did ordain as the Sabbath, he must sacrifice a good day's business in those communities where Christian majorities have closed shop on Sunday and made no exemption for the Sabbatarian. He cannot in some states buy birth control devices unless he alleges they are for hygienic reasons and then if he uses them it is against the law. And in other states he cannot purchase a good "schnapps" with which to drown the entree—herring, of course—unless it is a whole bottle and that is too much for a good Jew to drink at any one time!

While it is true that the Jew has significant political power in the United States, if an issue should emerge in which religious groups differ with each other, and all are wielding their political power behind the scenes, then the Jew is surely to be outmaneuvered and outvoted. No wonder, then, that the Jew presses in this country for an absolute separation of church and state. Frankly, he trusts a secular more than a Christianized state; and he is particularly distrustful of that kind of Christianity characterized even by friendly critics as the sentimentalized, superficial, culture-Christianity so prevalent in today's America—which is, after all, all that could be upheld by the state.

Nevertheless, as I have suggested, Jews do not by religious belief hold to a concept of state as separate from or separated from religion and the synagogue. What counsel can I suggest, therefore, concerning the role of church and synagogue in the public order that makes sense in a pluralistic society and remains true to our belief that all men and nations must serve God and are under his judgment?

IV

It is important first to reiterate that while traditional Jewish theology has not at all dealt with the comparatively new situation of religious pluralism such as we confront in America, nevertheless, there are to be found in Jewish theology concepts that offer us a starting point. There is, for example, the conviction that the conscience of man must remain inviolate. Within the synagogue itself, the effort to codify Jewish belief always met with failure. In time the Jews considered it a matter of pride that dissent was granted freedom of expression; and the rabbis frequently settled an issue by declaring: "These *and* these are the words of the Lord."

Although belief could not be coerced, it was expected that behavior would reflect consensus. Even here, however, the Jews quickly recognized that there was something radically wrong if religion used the instrumentality of the sword to coerce moral behavior not compellingly crucial for the minimal workings of the social order. And every lapse from this view—where zealous priest-regents or state-supported religious courts dealt too loosely with the human conscience—is recognized to have been sin and error and to have occasioned worse hardship for the entire household of Israel.

The destruction of the Second Commonwealth, for example, is seen by some rabbinic historians as punishment for the enforced conversion of the Idumeans by the Hasmonean dynasty and the corruption of a bought priesthood that served more devotedly the purposes of the ruler than the will of God, as well as some other sins prevalent in that day.

Particularly in relation to the non-Jew did Judaism caution that the state could require of the other only that he conform to those basic irreducible ethical practices crucial for the functioning of the public order. In a classic rabbinic parable, Abraham is rebuked by God for having turned out of his house a traveling idolater who refused to make homage to the Lord. Says God to Abraham, "I have endured this man all of his life and I have not cast him aside. Can you not forbear him but a little while?"

The non-Jew is called upon to forgo murder, theft, licentiousness, but he is not required to observe or conform to those practices or ideals considered the particular privilege of the Jew. Thus while traditional theology did not admit of a distinction between secular and holy—all was holy—there were, however, areas of the lesser holy (*hol*—secular), and greater holy (*kodesh*—cultistically sanctified). Jews nevertheless did recognize that some values needed to be upheld by all men if the social order were to be maintained, whereas others were the particular obligation of the committed believer. Is it not exactly this need to define today the legislative requirements for the achievement of the public good as against the particular obligations of our sectarian commitments that challenges our most concerned religious leadership?

V

To make even more relevant this inadequate theological discourse to the consensus of present-day America, permit me to conclude this discussion with the following observations, some of which obviously derive from my Jewish faith. Others reflect a pragmatic judgment related to the sociology of present-day interreligious relations.

(1) The church and synagogue obviously shape public morality by informing the conscience of the believer. While

there is much evidence to suggest that religious nurture effectively influences political and social attitudes in some areas of life, there is also other evidence in greater abundance that in the area of public morality church members are no less prone to sin and waywardness than non-church members. This suggests to me the unredeemed nature of man, whether he attends church or not; and as well that the public consensus is also a significant informer of values. It is possible that a man outside of the church may be as moral as one in the fold, and as immoral. God has many ways of reaching his people. These social statistics do not in any wise, however, detract from the commission of the church to try to inform conscience and to speak to social problems. As I have indicated, this is the synagogue's duty before the Lord. It does suggest that we need to try constantly to make our witness more effective and more meaningful.

For example, the liturgically-informed life, it has been demonstrated, does influence moral behavior. There is always the need, however, for religious leaders to help the observant understand how their devotion does relate itself to specific problems in the social order. The obvious shortcoming of church leaders is that they have been too willing to speak in vague generalities, if at all, or to choose for a comforting quiet rather than open up for illumination and understanding issues that engender disturbing controversy. The church, for the sake of its pastoral mission, has frequently abandoned its prophetic obligation.

When the church does speak its mind, of course, it ought to do so with knowledge and skill; synagogue social action committees particularly have been remiss in this regard. We have written declarations uninformed by all the facts and we have cast our thoughts in the secular language of the political party. The church ought never speak on an issue in the area of public morality unless in so doing it helps the adherent understand with fresh insight a dogma, or a belief, maintained within the religious tradition of the church.

If the synagogue supports desegregation, for example, it is not alone because it has become the law of this land; but rather because that law is good and pleasing in the eyes of the Lord. Our task is not only to add strength to those who fight racism, but to help them understand how these actions fulfill the will of God.

(2) The church informs the conscience of the citizen through its teaching, and the citizen acts in society through all the political machinery available. But the power of the church need also be used, not only to proclaim, resolve, or declare its stand. As a fellowship in society, the church, too, needs act as church in influencing the public order. This creates at least two problems: (a) How to handle the adherent who refuses or dissents from the social teaching of the church? (b) How to behave toward other religious groups in the society who may hold to a differing judgment?

My answer to these questions speaks, I think, to the heart of the matter—that is, the church, in the end, after all, is not a political party. It is the church. Its methods, therefore, must above all reflect the genius of religion. Its methods must include judgment on behavior but love for the person, prayer for the soul, and the promise of forgiveness, honesty in proclamation and humility before the Lord.

I am suggesting that the church must always allow for God to act upon the heart of man within the church. Therefore, as I have indicated, in the synagogue we have permitted and even encouraged freedom to dissent. Not all need be bound by the social declarations of the rabbis, and judgment is not made by one man on the motivations and sincerity of the other. That is God's function. Nor will we compel conformity in behavior unless the "peace of the city" is clearly endangered.

The church must refuse the temptation to manipulate, to coerce, to bribe, to wheedle and deal, to engage in cloak and dagger conspiracy, to withhold love. For these are not the ways of God.

Furthermore, we must discipline ourselves in our enthusiasm, so that we call not upon the power of the state to enforce clearly sectarian purposes, particularly when others in good conscience significantly dissent. Public good rather than private aggrandizement should testify to our religious commitment.

I charge that we have not behaved in this fashion. All of us have been guilty of serving with greatest zeal our own narrow concerns rather than the public weal. Think, if you will, of Catholics who are more involved in propagandizing for influencing and wielding power to achieve a bus ride for parochial school children than foreign aid to new countries emerging out of darkness; or Protestants more emotionally aroused by the serving of alcoholic beverages on airplanes than negotiations for disarmament or—closer to home—the desegregation of the public school; or the Jewish organizations more exercised over whether a congressman will support a favorable Mid-East policy than where he stands on Algeria, medical care, or any other issue. And how many times have we threatened legislators, openly or behind the closed door, with loss of vote should they not come along with us on the one narrow specific issue that concerns our religious community at the moment.

Another kind of perspective is called for from the church—

one that puts the most important public issues first and other sectarian issues last, one that forbids us from wielding our powers recklessly, one that views the members of antagonistic religious groups with some measure of love and charity.

(3) Finally, religious leaders, acknowledging the plurality of our society, have an obligation to be in communication. We are not now adequately enough in conversation with each other. We hold to stereotyped conceptions of each other. We are misinformed. We understand not the motivations that compel the other to the position he maintains. Frankly, too, a significant part of our conflict has nothing to do with principle and a lot to do with concern for status and political power, old fears, and resentments. Religion has been too often misused to serve individual secular purposes.

I suggest that were the doors open to frank ongoing conversation on these public issues, we should discover in America a consensus where there now appears to be none; and understanding each other better we would handle disagreement with greater civility and charity.

No society can exist unless there is some public philosophy, some consensus on values worth preserving and communicating, some agreement that all men must obey the minimal standards of behavior the existence of which makes the just society achievable. It is our duty in conversation to seek to define that public morality, cherishing all the while in our own separate religious traditions those additional obligations we assume before the Lord. May he bless our effort with peace.

8

Conscience and Religious Liberty

AS AN AVID READER of Catholic publications, I bring
testimony that the Catholic press has demonstrated a maturity
that portends well the readiness of this great Church to confront man's human problems with resourcefulness and courage.

There are some in the hierarchy who have been disturbed
by lay-edited Catholic publications that have criticized long
standing traditions. Similarly there are some among the laity
who have been disturbed, as they have seen clergy-directed
Catholic publications open their columns to Jews and Protestants as well as to Catholics who differ with each other and
some with the bishop of the diocese. For there are some
Catholics, just as there are some in all faiths, for whom controversy among the religious is hard to endure and differences
between clergy and laity produce anxiety. Such persons cling
desperately to the stereotype of the Church as a perfectly
redeemed society where all is obedience and peace. And, in

the name of the perfection of a past tradition they would suppress human striving and cause the spirit to shrink. However, the Church in its human manifestation is neither perfect, nor free from sin. Rather the Church's faithful wander through time, striving after an at oneness with God, prayerfully seeking the fulfillment of His promises.

Allow me then as an outsider, particularly on this evening when we discuss conscience and freedom, to reassure you with the truth long ago declared by Rabbi Mendel of Kotz that "controversies in the name of Heaven, spring from the root of Truth."

Drawing further upon Jewish Biblical and rabbinic insight, I suggest that when the Catholic press responsibly welcomes and indeed stimulates inquiry into Church policy, allows for freedom of dissent, encourages laity and clergy to speak their minds, and invites even the non-Catholic to add his perspective, then the press may be demonstrating that God's covenant is not with the hierarchy alone, but rather with an entire people, and that God's People are not only those in the Church, but all in the world who seek after Him. Or at least so I would like to believe for the truth is that God's People are not yet all of one mind and thus, we cannot know God's truth unless we are willing to hear what the other has to say. I believe with the Jewish mystics that God's revelation is continuous. The sparks of His divinity are to be found among all peoples, nations, and colors. His truth is not confined to any one religion, race, or class of men. Rather, God speaks to all of us through man and in history. The living God speaks to our human condition through the words and deeds of all humankind. Only if we hear the other can we know what it is that "The Holy One, blessed be He," might be trying to tell us.

AN APPRECIATION OF FATHER
JOHN COURTNEY MURRAY

I hasten to express my gratitude at being able to share the platform this evening with one of America's most distinguished religious leaders, Father John Courtney Murray. He has helped us to realize that freedom may not be license, but neither can faith be coerced. Church and state need not be antagonistic to each other, but on the other hand they must ever be mindful of their separateness in function and purpose. Individual conscience must be respected, but the fulfilling of human rights must involve us in social responsibilities.

In the light of a long history of oppression inflicted by man on his brother in the name of religion, Father Murray's call to the Church to respect conscience and to assure liberty truly combines the paradoxical prophetic elements of judgment and healing. If the Church cannot demonstrate to a shrinking world how man can live in peace despite differences, then it will have nothing more to say to this world! Yet, at the same time, the call to responsibility comforts. For we know that when the Church acts in history it has available to it a power that can transform and provide new purpose to human effort. I am humbled, therefore, to be in the presence of this great teacher of men.

THE BLESSING OF
RELIGIOUS DIFFERENCES

There is an advantage I bring unto this discussion, as a rabbi and as a teacher among the Jews, that derives from the sad fact that through much of history Jews have been the victims of the Church's arrogance and intolerance.

In the past centuries Jews were compelled by churchmen to engage in disputations, to hear preachment derogatory of their faith, to pay tax in support of the church. Jews were restricted in their right to study holy texts and to build and repair their synagogues. Finally, zealous Christians were misled by a distorted conception of their faith into believing that they were acting out God's will when they brought untold harm and suffering upon the persons of Jews.

It is possible for me to participate in this evening's session only because we both realize that the Constantinian Age is dead, never again to be revived. We both know that religion cannot be coerced and that the church ought not cajole the state into establishing by law its sectarian morality. The church suffers when it permits its "holy things" to become tools of secular power.

I do not contend that the Jews have a peculiar wisdom with regard to this problem, nor a superior virtue. Jewish history both in ancient times and in this day suggests confusion and uncertainty. It is recorded in our annals, and in yours, that our Kings once joined together both sacerdotal and secular functions—and this was displeasing in the eyes of God. We wreaked violence upon our prophets, we forcibly converted the Idumenas, we excommunicated those whose philosophic views were considered heretical. Even in this day, Jews in such contrasting countries as the United States, England, and Israel have approached the juridical problem of the establishment of the church or the relation of the church to the state, or the role of religions in education, in sharply different ways. History and sociology explain these differences better than theology or Jewish religious law.

Nevertheless, the one overriding factor in our experience—and it is this that explains the contemporary posture of the

Jew on church-state issues more than anything else—is the fact that we have been the consistent stiff-necked *No-sayer* to the imperialistic efforts of Christians to christianize all of society by force or coercive law. This evening I hint at the past in our own histories not to provoke your guilt, for it is not your guilt I want, but rather your responsibility.

Whatever else I say this evening, I want at least this to be remembered:

We Jews, a small people who have outlived mighty kingdoms and celebrated the defeat of countless tyrants, have been preserved by God to this day, so that we might stand in judgment against any and all who think that Power makes Right. Furthermore, our presence in every part of the world, our "exile" as it were, coupled with an insistence on our right to our own integrity as Jews wherever we live, suggests that it might be God's will that men fashion their society in such ways, so that freedom of conscience be guaranteed, religious differences be permitted, and civic loyalty be sought only at the highest order of commitment to the public good and not through the imposition of a spiritual uniformity.

Perhaps what God is trying to tell us in this history of the Jewish encounter with other religious and civilizations, is that it is not necessary for all men to worship God in the same manner. What God may require of men is not that they offer their sacrifice at the same altar, but rather that they live their lives in relation to each other in His spirit of service and sacrifice.

The Scriptural passage in Malachi 1:11, "For from the rising of the sun even unto the going down of the same, My name is great among the nations; And in every place offerings are presented unto My name, Even pure oblations; For My name is great among the nations, Saith the Lord of Hosts," has been interpreted by the Council of Trent as a reference to a sacrifice contemporaneous with Malachi of the *Type* of the later New Testament Sacrifice of the Mass (page 1697, *The Old Testament*, Confraternity Version, Guild Press). In contrast, however, it is understood by Jewish commentators to mean that when offerings are brought by the heathens to their gods in purity of devotion they are in reality intended for God. As the revered Chief Rabbi Hertz explained, offerings which the heathen present to their gods when animated by a pure spirit, are offered indirectly to the God of Abraham, for the "Lord of the World" looks to the heart of the worshiper (page 339, *The Twelve Prophets*, Soncino Press).

The name by which we call upon God ought to remain, therefore private and ineffable. Civic authority need only be concerned with our behavior toward each other, whether we act as brothers or as enemies.

My presence as a Jew in your midst provides the occasion to ask these questions:

In what ways do I, as a Jew, and you as a Christian, make a unique contribution to the quality of human society despite our differences? On the other hand, what are the inevitable consequences for society that derive from our differences? Is religious pluralism a scandal or the occasion for spiritual enrichment?

If there were no Jews, what would the world be like; and if the world were all Jewish, what is it that we would miss because of your absence? What is our responsibility to each other as long as you are to remain Christian and I Jewish?

Putting the question this way, I propose that each of us as individual persons and as a member of a distinctive religious community have some special gift to offer life. At the same time, we must be honest enough to recognize our own human finitude, imperfection, and incompleteness. We must be humble enough to believe that the other also may have an ingredient to add to the quality of human existence and finally that our own lives can be enriched through communication with and involvement in the life of the other.

I am suggesting that the issue of conscience and freedom involve more than a discussion of the juridical "rights" of the "person" in error as against the rights of that "error" itself to be institutionalized in society. This indeed is a most significant issue; but through the example of the conflict between Jew and Christian I am trying to raise in question whether it is necessarily displeasing to God that He be understood and worshiped differently by men. Perhaps through the reality of religious pluralism in the world, God intends to compel all of us to have to contend with each other in such spiritual fashion as to deepen our moral sensitivity; to restrain ourselves in such disciplined fashion as to strengthen the quality of self-sacrifice; to extend ourselves beyond our sectarian community in such purposeful fashion as to provide momentum to the virtue of human service. In all this, to recognize that differences among men may not necessarily be scandalous, but rather may testify to God's grandeur. "How manifold are thy works, O Lord!"

I choose to believe that once we can affirm and allow for the other, even while witnessing to our own truth, we set in motion that process that enables us to speak, teach, learn from, and thereby to enrich each other. I do not consider it an obligation to overcome all human differences, nor am I certain as to how and in what ways God intends men to remain different throughout history, but of this I am certain:

I must live by God's truth according to my ability to comprehend it.

I must recognize that neither man nor society—and that includes the church and the synagogue—have yet been redeemed from the capacity of sin and error; therefore I must be humble and not arrogant. I must make room for the other even when his conception of truth offends me.

I must seek the peace of my neighbor, despite his error. I must remain open to new revelation and to a new understanding of God's word. I must trust God to vindicate my service as I seek to know Him through fellowship with other human beings whom He created in His image, even though they be different, unique, and individual.

SOME SPECIFIC PROBLEMS TOUCHING UPON RELIGIOUS FREEDOM

Having suggested a particular attitude toward religious pluralism, allow me to expand these insights by confronting them directly with four concrete issues upon which there is tension in Jewish-Christian relations.

(1) The Relation of Church and State

I am mindful that American Catholics from their very first participation in the life of this country affirmed as a matter of policy the wisdom of disestablishment, separation, religious freedom, and equality under the law.

John Carrol, first Bishop in the United States in 1784, seven years before the adoption of the First Amendment said: "We have all smarted heretofore under the lash of an established church and shall therefore be on guard against every approach to it . . . Freedom and independence acquired by the united efforts, and cemented by the mingled blood of . . . fellow citizens, should be equally enjoyed by all!"

John Purcell, Archbishop of Cincinnati, in 1870, observed ". . . our civil Constitution grants perfect liberty to every denomination of Christians . . . and I verily believe this was infinitely better for the Catholic religion than were it the special object of the state's patronage and protection; all we want is a free field and no favor . . ."

Finally, I recall the statement of the American hierarchy in anticipation of the Second Vatican Council, ". . . we know, first of all, the advantages which have come to the Church from living and growing in an atmosphere of religious and political freedom. The very struggle which the Church here has had to face has been responsible in large measure for the vitality which it has developed as it grew to maturity, unaided by political preference but unimpeded by political ties."

Nevertheless, many Catholics are heir to a history and a tradition that suggest that the state fulfills its obligation to God by maintaining a society, culture, and public morality under the spiritual authority of the Church; and particularly in countries where Catholics are the significant majority the state is also expected to protect the catholicized culture from encroachments or corruptions that may derive from competing religious revelations.

Jews, on the other hand, have found their freedom restricted in such an environment. They have insisted, therefore, upon as absolute a separation as possible between the secular instrumentalities of the state and the authority of the church. And in fact they have welcomed political authority that eschews any obligation to religion. Such is the position of most American Jews.

I believe that both positions paradoxically contain elements of truth and yet both are subject to error. The vision of

Zechariah 4:1-6 is corrective and informing. In that great vision, you will recall, the prophet sees a seven-branched golden candlestick which has an unfailing supply of oil. Above the candelabra is a bowl and to the right and left of it stand two olive trees. These trees feed the bowl with oil through two spouts, and the bowl supplies the oil to the candlesticks through seven pipes.

According to Jewish commentators, the menorah represents the community of Israel, which receives its Divine grace through the prince and priest, the civic and religious leaders of the community symbolized by the two olive trees. They note that the olive trees produce oil without human labor and provide an inexhaustible supply of oil to the lamp. Thus, it is made clear that God acts upon His People with munificent love, both through political and religious instrumentalities. Both are vessels of His will and come under His judgment. Thus, the American Jews are wrong who believe that the so-called "secular" is freed from a responsibility to God and His word, or that state and religion can ever be arbitrarily separated from each other.

Significantly, there were two olive trees, not one. Thus Catholics who fail to distinguish between the unique duties, powers, and purposes of the state as against the church are also in error.

Finally, Zechariah records God as declaring, "This is the word of the Lord unto Zerubbabel saying: Not by might nor by power, but by My spirit saith the Lord of Hosts." Jewish commentators suggest that God is here warning the political authority that He cannot establish the Kingdom by force or coercion. Or to put it into contemporary terms, the establishment of a society where justice prevails and human kindness is practiced, cannot be achieved by violence, but will result only from that degree to which the participants in society permit God's grace to shine forth in their behavior. If the prince is cautioned against the use of force to achieve righteousness, how much more so is the priest to be warned against coercion as a method for achieving religious commitment!

Zechariah teaches, therefore, that the role and authority of the prince and the priest are distinct, but that both are intended to serve God's will. May I be so bold in this ecumenical age as to suggest further that God's grace in history can be and in fact is mediated directly and very frequently outside of the Church's instrumentality. In a society where there are many churches, it is arrogant for any one church to believe that it is the only "olive tree" through whom God spiritually replenishes "the lamp of the community."

(2) The Problem of State Support for Religious Education

The responsibility of the state to support financially the church's right to educate is a problem that has provoked severe conflict among religious groups in many countries. Interestingly, almost all religious groups, when they have achieved power, have accepted the largesse of the state. None of us has been consistent in this regard.

If the Jewish community in the United States has bitterly opposed the use of tax funds in support of any religion, it is also true that in Israel religion has been encouraged and all religions have been supported through public funds with equal regard. It is not out of religious conviction, therefore, that American Jews have opposed the granting of public funds in support of church activity. Rather, their position represents a prudential judgment that the well-being of religion itself requires such a prohibition. American Jews have come to the conclusion that the church is most vital when it must depend upon the resources of its own membership. When parishioners, themselves, must give sacrificially of themselves in order to maintain the church, then they involve themselves more intensively in their religion. In America religion has achieved a stature in society and has become a force in our lives of profound significance, perhaps, in great measure, because we have had to support the church ourselves, rather than share that responsibility with government.

I hasten to offer my own opinion that religion in Israel will have an even greater significance when it frees itself from state favor.

Yet, on the other hand, in our ever-growing, more complex, urbanized, technological, soon-to-be-computorized society, it is impossible for religion to play the role it must within society without entering into cooperative relationships with the state. An *absolute* separation of church and state is impossible, and where it is practiced, as in Communist Russia, separation merely serves as the extension of the government's policy of hostility to religion.

I look with favor, therefore, and with great anticipation at that new experiment in which America is presently engaged: whereby the state provides services and materials to all its citizens without discrimination, and enlists the support of all institutions, including the church, in the battle against poverty and inequality and for excellence in education. But in providing these services, the state—by law—restrains itself from giving the church any direct financial grant, or gain of property, or control over public policy.

This new policy, in my view, is not just a compromise worked out by politicians to overcome religious obstacles in order to unfreeze public funds for social welfare. It holds the promise of being a constructive device by which church and state can help each other and cooperate with each other in the effort to achieve justice in society, and yet maintain in significant ways their separateness and individuality.

Certainly the lesson we must have learned from all of history, including too sadly the experience of the church in Nazi Germany, is that when the church becomes too closely identified with the political organs of the society, when it becomes dependent financially on that society, it is bankrupt. It is silent when it should be prophetic. Therefore, even as the church cooperates and takes assistance from the state, it must do so with restraint and self-discipline, and only to that degree that it is serving the public purpose.

(3) *Religious Morality and Public Law*

I believe it proper and right for the church in the exercise of its prophetic function to seek changes in the social order, to make pronouncements, to inspire its faithful and itself to act in corporate fashion in order to achieve just law. Indeed, I applaud those churchmen who, in the name of a Higher Law, have been willing to suffer abuse, face imprisonment, even risk death, as they protest local and state statutes that are patently unjust and inhuman.

Yet, the church is not a political organization. It ought not be a political party. Whenever the church, as church, has attempted to wield political power on a sustained and institutionalized basis, the consequences for freedom have been disastrous. State power sanctified by indiscriminating corporate church support produces the vilest form of spiritual corruption.

Where else will the state in an unredeemed and corruptible world find the resources to correct itself and to advance freedom if the church becomes an active partner in maintaining the status quo arrangement? The church needs to be ever alert to act upon God's word of judgment on man's creations; and so, even though we are in and of society, we must self-consciously direct our eyes and hearts to the eternal Master of the world.

It is this realization that revelation is continuous, that justice needs ever to be advanced, that life is dynamic and requires always new law, new understanding, that the Word itself demands new interpretation and new application, that ought inhibit us against presuming at any one time, that civil laws of morality can be legislated in final and fixed form. Particularly when men, in good conscience through various religious commitments, disagree sharply with each other in their conception of morality, it behooves the church to restrain itself.

I wish to commend and to applaud the policy suggested by Cardinal Cushing of Boston with regard to a controversy there over the right of physicians and pharmacists to furnish birth control devices. He testified: "It does not seem reasonable for me to forbid in civil law a practice that can be considered a matter of private morality." Cardinal Cushing's insistence that there is a distinction between civil and moral law, between public and private morality, his repudiation in principle of "a resort to the coercive instrument of law to enforce upon a whole community moral standards that the community does not commonly accept" is worthy of serious consideration by churchmen everywhere and by all religious groups.

Scripture offers us guidance here also. The prophet is to be known not by his claim to revelation, but rather by the truth of his works. This suggests to me that in a pluralistic society the church must make its case for law in the civic order, not by invoking its spiritual authority or by exercising secular power. Rather through persuasion and reason it must demonstrate the consequences of its position and that of the alternative proposals, and through such demonstration win the free consent of the citizenry.

Furthermore, Scripture calls upon Israel to be a "light unto the nations" by accepting for itself the yoke of Torah. Through self-discipline, through the adherence of the Israelites to God's Word, the Holy People will demonstrate that God's Word is a law for all men. Thus, they will set an example for others to follow and inspire men to call upon God's name.

I am suggesting that the church seek first the loyalty and discipline of its faithful; secondly, that it be ready to join with all others in the repair of the world; but thirdly, that where men in good conscience differ with each other, it be careful only to use the weapons of the spirit, namely, example and witness, rather than the coercive power of the state.

(4) On the Relations Between Jews and Christians

This leads me to the fourth issue and that is our hope for each other as Jews and Christians; for I believe that our eschatological vision will determine significantly the character of our contemporaneous relationship and influence the degree to which we can live and work together in trust or suspicion. Time does not permit me to say all that I wish, or ought, before such a distinguished gathering, but allow me please these concluding words:

There is no doubt in my mind that the overwhelming

majority of the world's Catholic hierarchy repudiate anti-Semitism in all its forms and eschew any restrictions on the liberty of Jews. Most particularly I commend the leaders of the American Church for their vigorous and forthright action at the Vatican Council. Patriarch Maximos has unfairly maligned the American Church when he suggested that the American prelates voted for the Declaration on the Jews "for personal reasons," that is, as he explained out of "a sentiment of pity due to the massacre of millions of Jews by Nazism" and "due to the fact that the great number of Americans have commercial interests with Jews." This is a calumny against the integrity of the American hierarchy and it should be everywhere repudiated! I am satisfied that American churchmen have acted out of conviction and in proper understanding of their own faith commitment.

But I must add, sadly, by reason of the doubt that still exists concerning the ultimate wording of the Statement that Jews everywhere will be sorely distressed if the Church does not at long last issue a word of reconciliation.

Jews do not ask for, nor will they accept your "forgiveness" for having rejected your Christology. Without raising in question the correctness or error of your interpretations of the promises of the prophets, it is enough for me to assert that in our view we believe we have been faithful to God's law. Indeed, He has been our savior and protector through a long and brutal history. We have suffered, yes, but not because we are "accursed" or "rejected of God" nor as punishment for the sin of "deicide." But rather, because of man's sinfulness and his failure to do the will of a loving God.

Not only do we not seek your forgiveness, but neither can you "absolve" us of the crime of the crucifixion. For the Jews collectively of that day, and certainly of this day, bear no *special* guilt in that regard.

The fact that Jews, Romans, and the disciples were participants in the tragedy ought to suggest that all men bear a collective responsibility for evil wherever it may occur on earth, for humankind is one and we are each of us responsible for the other.

Yet distressing assertions are still to be heard from Catholics. Patriarch Maximos declared: "There certainly remains on the forehead of the Jewish people, as long as it is far from Christ the Redeemer, what the prophets of the Old Testament prophesied: A stain of shame." And even more provocative was the declaration of the Bishop of Signe, Luigi Maria Carli, who asserted in his review for the Italian Catholic clergy, "I consider it legitimate to affirm that the *entire* Jewish people at the time of Christ was responsible collectively for deicide, although only the leaders, together with a section of their followers, materially committed the crime . . . In this sense and according to the Biblical way of thought, Judaism after the time of Jesus has also, objectively, participated in the responsibility for deicide, to the extent that this Judaism constitutes the free and voluntary continuation of the Judaism of those times." For these same reasons, states Bishop Carli, the Jews can be called "reprimanded" and "accursed of God."

Confusion over the theological teaching of the Church on this issue will be resolved only when we hear from the Ecumenical Council a word of clarification and reconciliation acknowledging that men have misinterpreted and misused Christian teaching and repudiating all those who still do.

I would not wish to dwell on the past at all except to warn you that how the Church confronts its own past contribution to the creation of a climate in which anti-Semitism could have flourished and still exists, will determine in great measure how well you will root out of your own soil the stinking weed of Jew-hatred. The honesty with which the Church confronts its own shortcoming and error will determine the degree to which the Church can be a healing and reconciling influence in civilization.

In the meantime, it is clear that Catholics and Jews have already begun to talk to each other and to work together for justice and peace, and this is good. For indeed God has promised that He will be present when men gather together to work in His name.

Yet I must confess that there are some Jews who are wary of too intimate an involvement with Catholics. Some Jews remain uncertain to what degree the Catholic's cooperative and friendly demeanor masks an intent to convert us and to bring us to the Christian's truth. This returns me, you see, to my introductory remarks. For I raise in question whether one can maintain over any length of time, sincerely and firmly a commitment to religious liberty if he does not allow for the grounds and the truth of the other.

When the Jews invoke Zephaniah's dream that God in His time "will turn to the peoples a pure language that they may all call upon the name of the Lord, to serve him with one consent" (Zephaniah 3:9), we do not understand this to mean that the distinctiveness of peoples will disappear, nor that all men will become Jews. Rather we hope that all men, brothers in spirit, will engage together in the work of righteousness, thus serving God with one shoulder, as it were, as though joined to one yoke.

Not all Jews accept this interpretation. There are some Jews of exclusivist bend of mind—just as there are exclusivists in the Church—who have defined their existence as Israel or as the New Israel in such delimiting terms as to prohibit all others from the promises and responsibility of God's election, unless they fulfill certain racial or creedal qualifications.

I prefer, however, those rabbinic masters who recognized that he is worthy to be called Israel who has these three signs: "Being compassionate, humble, and charitable" (Yebamoth 79A).

I invoke the rabbinic commentary on Psalm 146:8, "The Lord loveth the righteous," where the sage explains, "The Lord loves the righteous because righteousness is not a matter of heritage or family." He adds, "You will find that the priests form a caste, as it were, and the Levites form a caste. For it is said, 'Oh *House* of Aaron, bless ye the Lord; Oh *House* of Levi, bless ye the Lord (Psalm 135:19–20).'

"A man may wish to become a Priest or a Levite and yet he cannot. And why? Because his father was neither a priest nor a Levite.

"But if a man, Jew or Gentile, wishes to be righteous, he can do so because the righteous cannot form a House. Therefore it is said: '*Ye* that fear the Lord, bless ye the Lord (Psalm 135:20)!' It is not said House of those that fear the Lord, for the righteous form no father's house. Of their own free will they have come forward and loved the Holy One, blessed be He, and that is why He loves them (Numbers Rabba 8:2)."

I suggest that if we but recognize that righteousness is within the capacity of all men, whatever their house, their station in life, their color, their nationality, even their religion, if we but fear God and live our lives as a blessing to God, then we will have discovered that answer which justifies and explains the importance of conscience and the value of religious freedom.

9

~~~~~~

Theological Issues
in Jewish-Christian Relations

DURING THE EICHMANN TRIAL in Jerusalem, one of
America's Protestant editors observed that while "Pagans
inaugurated and implemented the Nazi crimes against Jewry,
Christians stood by and accepted them uncritically." The editor then asked:

> Could the Nazi persecutions have been perpetuated with-
> out a long-standing atmosphere of anti-Jewish attitudes
> in which the Christian community has subscribed? Be-
> cause the Jews had cut themselves off from Jesus of
> Nazareth, had the Christians in turn severed them from
> the bond of humanity (*Christianity Today*, Nov. 10,
> 1961)?

This editor wisely realized that even though anti-Semitism
today rarely invokes religious sentiment to justify itself, even

though it is based on pseudo-scientific theories of race or paranoiacally induced hypotheses of a Jewish-Communist-Zionist international conspiracy, and even though it serves ends that are clearly secular—psychological, economic, and political—Jew-hatred can still find a receptive response in western civilization. The human heart for two thousand years has been encouraged to favor it.

Jews are quick to point out that this stimulation of contempt for the Jew has been the chief responsibility of Christian churchmen, who interpreted their Scripture and formulated their theological teachings in such a way as to suggest that the Jews are an accursed people, destined forever to suffer evil until they will have accepted Jesus as the Christ promised in their own Jewish Testament. As the noted French Jewish historian, Jules Isaac, has written:

> Christian anti-Semitism is a powerful millenary and strongly rooted trunk upon which (in the Christian world) all other varieties of anti-Semitism are grafted, even those of a most anti-Christian nature.

In a recent survey conducted at the behest of the Anti-Defamation League, social researchers at the University of California discovered that more than half of America's Christians believe the Jews are "most responsible for crucifying Christ," and almost the same number believe the Jews "can never be forgiven until they accept Jesus as the true savior." It is such a teaching of collective Jewish responsibility for the crucifixion that still fertilizes the soil for the ugly stock that is anti-Semitism.

Most Christians in America, and particularly liberal Protestants—whose church-school texts, Bible commentaries, and sermons have displayed recently a remarkable degree of sensitivity—are shocked at the suggestion that Christian teaching could be responsible for fomenting such hatred. After all, does not the New Testament itself teach that "God is love and he who abides in love, abides in God and God abides in him . . . If anyone says 'I love God' and hates his brother, he is a liar. For he who does not love his brother whom he has seen, cannot love God, whom he has not seen." Furthermore, does not Christian Scripture teach that Jesus himself called upon God to forgive those who crucified him "for they know not what they do?" Finally, does not Paul teach that even though the Jews are enemies of the Gospel, their election by God still endures? Jews are beloved for the sake of the forefathers. "To the Jews belong the Sonship, the glory, the covenants, the giving of the law, the worship and the promises . . . and the gifts and call of God are irrevocable."

Without doubt, it is a *distortion* of Christian teaching to accuse it of a responsibility for anti-Semitism. Yet the facts are that such a distorted conception of Christianity was religion taught by the most sainted and revered of church fathers, priests, bishops, and popes, and after the Reformation, by some of the leaders of Protestant Christianity.

If one fails to view the whole New Testament in its *entirety* and selects carefully certain passages hostile towards Jews and Judaism, without the clarifying restrictions these passages must receive from other passages—in other words, if one reads the New Testament carelessly or with evil intent, then it is possible to use Christian Scripture as a source for anti-Semitism. This is how the New Testament has been *misused* through many centuries. No wonder, then, that Reverend Charles H. Buck, Jr., Dean of the Episcopal Cathedral of St.

Paul in Boston, felt obliged to confess: The basic document of anti-Semitism in the Western world is the New Testament." Reverend A. Roy Eckhardt, distinguished editor of the *Journal of Bible and Religion,* was moved to warn: "Until the church admits concertedly and goes out of its way to proclaim that there are roots of anti-Semitism in its own Scriptures, Christian anti-Semitism will not be overcome."

Thus, the very first thing that Jews hope Christians will do in the fight against anti-Semitism is to make sure that proper explanations and commentaries are provided at all times, when those passages in the New Testament are read that might lend themselves, if not properly understood, to Jew-hatred.

As I have indicated, perverse theological formulations based on such a faulty reading of Christian Scripture, have been part of a long history and tradition of Christian teaching. According to these formulations:

Jews, by rejecting Jesus as the promised Christ, rejected God. Misled by the corrupt teachings of their hypocritical leaders, the Pharisees and scribes, the Jews were blinded to God's truth and, in bloodthirsty fashion, they crucified the Savior. As a consequence, God established a new covenant with all those, Jews and gentiles, who believed in Jesus. He formed a New Israel from these believers and they displaced the Israel of old as God's elect people. Furthermore, as prophesied, the Jews, by virtue of their iniquity, were exiled from the land, their temple was destroyed, they were made to suffer punishment, endure poverty, and serve the Christian as a slave people. Only by accepting Jesus as Christ can Jews find salvation.

With a bizarre logic many Christians believed that by adding to the Jews' misery they were fulfilling God's will and, in fact, some believed that if the Jew were made miserable enough, he might abandon his Jewishness and convert to Christianity. Protestant scholars, even in this day, are capable of describing such a policy as followed by Martin Luther, for example, as one of "sharp kindheartedness."

Martin Luther, in a fashion not unlike Christian leaders who preceded him, taught that by rejecting Christ the Jews revealed a hatred for God. Thereby they lost their status as a chosen people. To the degree that they persisted in their Jewishness, they became demonic, "the mouthpiece of the devil." "To tolerate the rejection of the Gospel," Luther warned, "would be merely to fix them more firmly in their errors." He called for the razing of their houses, the burning of their synagogues, the confiscation of Jewish prayer books and Talmuds, and their enforced servitude. "They must be forced through their misery . . . to profess that the Messiah has come, and he is our Jesus."

Jews hope, therefore, that the second thing that Christians will do in the fight against anti-Semitism is to repudiate any such perverse conceptions within Christian theology that might still seem to justify a hatred of the Jew.

This second request, however, will not be so easy to accomplish, since this theology of contempt consists of many components, some of which touch the core of Christian thought; and Christian theologians have not yet worked out new ideas to replace these reprehensible ones. How difficult it is for some Christians to face up to the Jewish problem is to be seen by the fact that the Catholic bishops at the Vatican Council, after three sessions, still remain divided on what to say about the Jews and how to say it. (Since this was written, of course, the Vatican Council issued a forthright statement decrying anti-Semitism and rejecting any interpretation of Scripture that would view Jews as rejected or accursed. In failing to define the meaning of God's ongoing relationship with the Jews, however, the statement was considered by some Jews as inadequate).

Protestants affiliated with the World Council of Churches and the National Council of Churches, have already issued declarations that speak to some of these issues: As early as 1948 the World Council of Churches, meeting in Amsterdam, Holland, confessed that "the churches in the past have helped to foster an image of the Jews as the sole enemies of Christ, which has contributed to anti-Semitism in the secular world." In 1961 at New Delhi, India, the World Council of Churches added this directive regarding Christian teaching:

> . . . The historic events which led to the crucifixion should not be so presented as to fasten upon the Jewish people of today responsibilities which belong to our corporate humanity, and not to one race or community.

On June 5, 1964, the General Board of the National Council of Churches confessed that "sometimes as Christians we have given way to anti-Semitism. We have even used the events of the crucifixion to condemn the Jewish people . . ."

It is clear that American Protestants certainly: (1) Will oppose any effort made by any church to impose its religion on others or to seek conversion through the use of force, pressure, or intimidation, whether exercised with the assistance of state power or utilized by the church alone: (2) Will repudiate as a valid Christian teaching any suggestion that the Jews are an accursed or reprobate people by virtue of the crucifixion.

In recent years, also, Christian scholars have come to recognize that the religion of the Jews at the time of Jesus was not a degenerate, outward, hypocritical display of ceremonialism or legalism. Pharasaic Judaism attained to a high level of ethical sensitivity and, in fact, within rabbinic teaching one can find most of the insights of Jesus' social and ethical philosophy as well as his criticism of hypocrisy. The Christian claim does not have to be based on a derogation of Judaism, but rather on the unique, once-and-for-all-times redeeming significance of the incarnation.

Christian scholars have also realized that the Jewish Bible has a message of its own. It must not be read merely as a text providing Scriptural authority for the belief that Jesus is the Christ, nor as the source of a religion that prepared the way for and remains inferior to Christianity. In describing God's dealings with the Jewish people, the Jewish Bible reveals lessons and insights about God and man that can provide a wisdom with which to clarify human problems even of this day. The Jewish Bible has a value and a contemporaneity so unique in the world's literature as to make it worthy of reverence and diligent study. Without the Jewish Bible, the Gospels would provide only a partial and incomplete witness. Christianity needs the corrective and supplementary understandings of the Hebrew Scripture.

The growing acceptance of such convictions is a significant and meaningful step forward in the reconciliation between Jew and Christian. But they leave unanswered, still, a whole host of additional questions, confrontation with which is required if we are to attain to a fuller measure of interreligious understanding. I hasten to admit that these questions are directed both to the Jew and the Christian. Furthermore, in answering these questions, both of us must be ready to accept the pain of disagreement, even as we search for the ways of

living and working together for the common good. A most
heartening thing about the present situation is that Jews and
Christians are beginning to meet one another in dialogue sessions, in shared study of Biblical text, at the seminary level,
and in the community. One can only anticipate, therefore,
that we shall soon see emerging a new understanding, a new
theology of the nature of the Jewish-Christian relationship.

For example, Christians have already acknowledged that
Christianity has its roots in a Judaism of old; but what significance is there in the Judaism that has developed since the
biblical period? What can Christians learn about God's truth
from His continuous and contemporaneous dealings with the
Jewish people?

Jews on their part have to consider what it is that God
might be trying to communicate through His gracious dealings with Christians. What is the significance of the fact that
these people consider themselves Israel and heir to the promises of Abraham? Are they not covenanted to the same God
revealed in the Jewish Biblical testimony? Have they not extended God's Word to the four corners of the earth; and by
their sacrificial witness and acts of charity have they not
brought some knowledge of God's truth to men and nations?
What is it that Jews can learn from Christians?

Both Jews and Christians together need to face the fact that
in their conflict with an aggressive modern form of secularism
and atheism, the theocentric faith of both is under attack.
Furthermore, a failure of Judaeo-Christian faith to develop a
healing relationship with the hungry and exploited of our over-
populated, racially-divided world will strengthen those who
suggest that the religion of Israel, whether Old or New, is
irrelevant.

Thus, even as Christian and Jew develop a theology that

will allow for and explain God's relation to the other, so both also need to act upon that which they share together, in order to relate themselves meaningfully to the world.

The way in which Jews and Christians will respect each other's integrity will enable both of them better to face the world. Similarly, the fraternity we experience as we cooperate together in serving the world, may provide us with a deeper understanding, individually, of what it means to call one's self Israel.

Finally, the time has come, I think for the Christian to stop trying to convert the Jew. It is far better for us to talk and listen to each other, learn from and teach each other in a spirit of mutual respect and esteem.

Thus I commend the resolution of the General Board of the National Council of Churches, which urged:

That the members of its constituent communions seek that true dialogue with the religious bodies of the Jewish community through which differences in faith can be explored within the mutual life of one family of God— separated, but seeking from God the gift of renewed unity—knowing that in the meantime God can help us find our God-forgiven unity in the common service of human kind.

10

The Mission of the Jews

A FOREWORD ON THE NATURE OF THE
JEWISH-CHRISTIAN DIALOGUE

NEVER BEFORE in history have Jews and Christians really confronted each other as brothers, each entitled to the dignity of his uniqueness, both respectful of the other's freedom of conscience and right to be. We can at last talk with each other now, in honesty and without fear, because we both sense, somehow, that God will address us through the other. We are attentive and will listen, thus true dialogue is possible.

In the past, Jewish-Christian confrontation was fraught with danger and physical violence. Both the New Testament and testimonies of Jewish history record a tragic tale of man's oppression of his brother because of religious difference. The truth is we have never really spoken words to each other—we persecuted, flogged, burnt at the stake, humiliated, mocked, murdered, feared, and hated the other. Now guilt and suspicion have made it difficult to converse even when we wish it.

That some Jews will resist conversation with Christians whose categories of thought in relation to the Jews are shaped by Paul's language and are evangelically oriented, is a fact that must be recognized before dialogue can begin. But it is proper to put this fact itself under scrutiny and to examine the reasons for the Orthodox Jewish attitude and to deal with it if we can. I believe that the Jewish resistance is not only an understandably defensive reaction to past Christian aggression, but that it reflects an Hebraic uneasiness with the facile handling of theology by Christians who have adopted Greek concepts of knowledge. The very request that we define ourselves for you in the philosophic categories of Western thought is reason for reservation in the Jewish community. I think it proper to point out, however, that none of us in God's one-world can describe ourselves properly except in relation to the other, nor can we expose ourselves to history without facing the possibility of revision in attitudes.

At any rate, anyone who is sensitive to the fast-changing events of our world will realize that old categories of thought and the usual ways of perceiving ourselves have been challenged. Our obligations toward each other, and for all men everywhere, require more openness and less defensiveness. It requires at least the willingness, despite our differences and our alleged designs on each other, to explore together opportunities to improve this world. So we have to talk to each other without the restraint of inhibiting guidelines, without fear and suspicion; but we must be honest and frank with each other.

I cannot help but call to mind the challenging revolutionary address delivered by Catholic Bishop Blomjous of Tanganyika, East Africa, who contemplates the tension between a new concept of "ecumenism" and the traditional concept of evangelization. He writes:

We used to think that the Church was sent into the world to gain the adherence of all men to Christ and that her missionary effort was destined to convert all men to live as brothers in a single church. While we realized that this aim was not to be achieved in our lifetime, we did feel through our missionary effort we hastened the coming of this day. Today, however, we are faced with the realization that pluralism and specifically religious pluralism is established in most parts of the world and that the forces of history will eventually make it a universal phenomenon.

Sober statistics tell us that Christians represent a smaller percentage of the world population in every decade. With the shrinking globe, moreover, we can no longer speak of any uniformly Christian area or country in the sense that the Christian church and national culture are coextensive.

It seems that religious pluralism is part of God's plan. Can we still assert that the Lord has sent His Church into the world to gather all men in the unity of faith? We are forced to ask ourselves the serious question, what is the theological meaning of religious pluralism, what is God attempting to tell us through the multiplicity of religions?

The original schism between the Jews and the Jewish-Nazarenes represents in history a prototype of division among brothers, each faithful to God in his own way. In this modern world in which we live we still have to resolve that conflict.

Is it too much to expect that when we leave here this week our understanding of each other will take on a meaning profounder and far more significant than could have been anticipated had either of us rejected, out of hand, the occasion for agape? There is a rabbinic maxim, which Matthew recasts (Matthew 18:20), "Where two or three are gathered together to discuss Torah, God's presence is among them." You have invited me to address you on my understanding—a Jew's understanding of himself and the mission of his people—and I am here. Praised be to God. Now to begin.

THE BIBLICAL PERSPECTIVE

The Biblical text that most accurately defines and shapes the Jew's conception of himself and his mission is God's declaration to Moses:

> Now, therefore if you will obey My voice and keep My covenant, you shall be My own possession among all peoples; for all the earth is Mine and you shall be to Me a kingdom of priests and a holy nation. (Exodus 19:5–6).

It is not with an arrogant self-righteousness nor with any sense of racial or physical superiority that we read this text. We did not choose God; He chose us. One ironic rabbinic legend elaborates that God lifted Sinai, held it over the heads of a reluctant people, and threatened them with oblivion if they would not accept His law. The people shouted out their affirmation of life and replied, "We shall do and we shall be obedient" (Shabbat 88a, 129b; Abodah Zarah 2).[1] God

---

[1] Other legends, of course, suggest that Israel accepted the Torah without coercion. One, in fact, records that God offered the Torah first to every tribe and nation. Each turned it down, unwilling to accept the discipline of the Commandments. Whereupon Israel pointed out to God that their patriarchs had already observed the Law before it was even formally revealed. They answered in one voice "All that the Lord has spoken will we do and be obedient" (Abodah Zarah 2b).

shaped and disciplined this unruly, stiff-necked, slave people, the poorest of nations and made them His treasured people among all peoples. We now know that we cannot live outside of God's law. Were we to be unfaithful to Him, life would be without meaning. Our survival as a people is dependent upon our loyalty to the covenant and is testimony to God's graciousness and fidelity. Our mission is to be, as best we can, what God chose us to be—a kingdom of priests and a holy nation.

The Biblical text assures us that God is Lord over all nations and the Author of all history, "for all the earth is Mine." The people Israel can make no exclusive claim on God's love, nor consider his graciousness to us of extraordinary character nor act as though by the election we were superior to the law that governs all men: "Are you not like the Ethiopians to me, O People of Israel, says the Lord. Did I not bring up Israel from the land of Egypt and the Philistines from Caphtor and Aram from Kir. Behold the eyes of the Lord God are upon the sinful kingdom and I will destroy it from the surface of the ground, except that I will not utterly destroy the house of Jacob, says the Lord" (Amos 9:7–8).

It is then God's doing not ours that the people of Israel have been chosen to be God's servant (Isaiah 42:1–6), His witnesses (Isaiah 43:12), the instrumentality by which His salvation is to reach the ends of the earth (Isaiah 49:6).

But God has not used us in any impersonal or mechanical way. To become involved in God's purpose is to know the warmth and compassion of His love. The Bible speaks of God as Father (Isaiah 62:15, 64:8, Psalms 68:5, 103:13). We are His first born (Exodus 4:22), His son (Psalms 2:7). In His love for us, He is like a husband, "And I will betroth you to Me forever. I will betroth you to Me in righteousness and

Justice, in steadfast love and in mercy. I will betroth you to
Me in faithfulness and you shall know the Lord (Hosea
2:19–20).[2]

"How odd of God to choose the Jews" the philosopher
ponders. But is it not exactly to teach us that God's methods
contradict every pagan conception of power and grandeur? A
slave people, a mixed multitude without access to physical
power—this is the people God uses.

The history of Israel instructs us that God is there with the
meek and oppressed of our world. Like a flaming bush not
consumed, God inflames the hearts of men, inspiring them to
seek freedom and fullness in life. God is with us—indeed He
is with all men—who accept upon themselves the yoke of the
kingdom of heaven, who strive after truth and seek wisdom,
who pursue peace and establish righteousness.

A slave people are given the power to speak to the consciousness of mankind because they bear on their flesh the
marks of man's inhumanity. The divine character of the
Exodus is to be seen not only in the fact that this slave people
sought emancipation, but also in that the Hebrews were given

[2] The liturgy of the Rosh Hashanah summarizing this Biblical perspective sings:
    "We are Thy people and Thou art our God
     We are Thy children and Thou our Father
     We are Thy servants and Thou our Master
     We are Thy congregation and Thou our Portion
     We are Thine inheritance and Thou our Lot
     We are Thy flock and Thou our Shepherd
     We are Thy vineyard and Thou our Keeper
     We are Thy work and Thou our Creator
     We are Thy faithful and Thou our Beloved
     We are Thy loyal ones and Thou our Lord
     We are Thy subjects and Thou our King
     We are Thy devoted people and Thou our Exalted God."

the spiritual strength to transform the natural logical instinct of men to identify with the oppressor and to work out their aggression by becoming masters over others. Torah legislation commits Israel to champion the cause of the widow and orphan, the stranger, the homeless, the naked, to establish justice in society as evidence of God's love for mankind. No other justification for this mission is required than the reminder "For ye were strangers in the land of Egypt." But if God's chosen instrument is a stiff-necked slave people, then we can be assured that history will record the pain and suffering, the anguish that is required of men before history can be redeemed.

On the one hand, Israel and the Jewish people will exemplify man's continual rebellion against the yoke of the Law; and on the other hand, Israel, not for any sins of her own, will endure the hatred of all men who refuse to recognize the oneness and singularity of God. Israel will personify the struggle of man to overcome waywardness, who must suffer punishment for his transgressions; but Israel will also symbolize the innocent man who suffers unjustly because of the transgressions of others.

Indeed, Jews were chosen by God, but man is free to rebel, to follow the stirrings of his flesh and to choose his own ways. Although we are called upon, to return the gift of God's love by faithfulness, too late some of us realize that obedience to God is genuine freedom and that we attain to the full dimension of our humanity only when we pattern our lives after His holiness.

Sons of Israel have often rebelled against God, and whenever a people transgress against God's law they are sure to be scourged. But Israel is assured, and through us all mankind may know, that God is merciful, forgiving, and faithful "For I have no pleasure in the death of anyone, says the Lord God, so turn and live" (Ezekiel 18:32).[3]

Just as within the camp of Israel we have had to struggle with the challenge of obedience and redemption, so too each nation and all nations have had to confront God's requirements for righteousness and His promise of peace. The nations' treatment of Israel have served as an index of their humanity. When men reject God they inflict their anger upon His servant.[4]

Feudal lords, Christian princes, the Holy Crusaders, the Czars of Russia, Nazi pagans, Communist atheists, Arab nationalists—all these have offended against God's people. Western civilization records its own stiff-necked rebellion against God by a shameful testimony of pogroms, expulsions, teaching of contempt, inquisitions, and at last, brutal mass murder. Shocked by the horrendous treatment of Jews, our

[3] "I am He Who blots out your transgressions for My own sake and I will not remember your sins" (Isaiah 43:25).

". . . The King of Nineveh . . . made proclamation . . . yea, let everyone turn from his evil way and from the violence which is in his hands. Who knows, God may yet repent and turn from His fierce anger so that we perish not. When God saw what they did, how they repented from their evil way, God repented of evil which He had said He would do to them, and He did not do it" (Jonah 3:6–10).

The Prophet Jeremiah assures us that God's covenant with His people Israel is forever and that in His own time, God will redeem all our strivings: "Behold the days are coming, says the Lord, when I shall make a new covenant with the House of Israel and the House of Judah. . . . I will put My law within them and I will write it upon their hearts and I will be their God and they shall be My people . . . for I will forgive their iniquity and I will remember their sin no more. Thus says the Lord, Who gives the sun for light by day and the fixed order of the moon and the stars for light by night, Who stirs up the sea so that its waves roar—the Lord of Hosts is His name: if this fixed order departs from before Me, says the Lord, only then shall the descendants of Israel cease from being a nation before Me forever.

civilization has the opportunity at last to cleanse itself and to understand the nature of human responsibility. No longer can we turn our back on our brother, stand idly by at human injustice, treat any minority with indignity, or permit any dictator, political party, or human institution to become a substitute for the Lordship of God. It may yet be that by the stripes inflicted upon the Jews, men and nations will be healed.

SOME IMPLICATIONS OF THIS BIBLICAL PERSPECTIVE FOR JEWISH-CHRISTIAN DIALOGUE

Torah

The Jewish mission requires that the Jew remain disciplined to the Law, "If you will obey My voice." Torah provides us a way of life that links our human striving to God's

---

Thus says the Lord: If the heavens can be measured and the foundations of earth below can be explored, only then will I cast off all the descendants of Israel for all that they have done, says the Lord" (Jeremiah 31:31–37).

(Cf. The New Testament view that Israel remains God's people despite their unbelief in Jesus as the Christ. "What if some were unfaithful. Does their faithlessness nullify the faithfulness of God. By no means!" (Romans 3:3). "I ask then, has God rejected his people. By no means!" (Romans 11:1).

[4] In an interpretation of the phrase "For I am love-sick" (Canticles 2:5), the rabbis explained: "Master of the universe, all the ills You bring upon me—are to bring me to love You the more." Another interpretation: "All the ills the nations of the world bring upon me, are because I love You" (Canticles Rabbah 2:14).

"When trouble comes into the world, Israel feels it first; when good comes, Israel feels it first" (Lamentations Rabbah 2:3).

Israel has been despised and rejected by men—a people of sorrows acquainted with grief, afflicted, wounded because of the transgressions of others. By oppression and judgment our people have been taken away though we did no violence, nor was there deceit in our mouth (Isaiah 53).

eternal purpose. It enables man to sanctify the flesh and to
direct lusts and appetites, ambition and pride into behavior
that enhances life, that serves the living and pleases the Creator.[5] It enables us to respond to God's voice, for we believe
that God expects us to translate our vision of Him, our most
sacred ideals and our noblest values into a concrete expression of man's love for God and fellow man by the enactment
of just laws and the building of a righteous society.

In an unredeemed world, there can be neither justice, nor
salvation without law.

God provides us, by His grace, the wisdom and the will to
justify our lives and His purpose for us through the discipline
of Torah.

Until the end of time, man must continue to grow toward
perfection, wholeness, and peace (Sholom which means
peace, also means completeness, wholeness, at-oneness). Life
under the Law assists man in that growth. Men must participate in and create society; and society, too, needs to be governed by law.

In the centuries-old debate over whether man is "justified"
before the Lord by faith or through devotion to the Law,
Judaism has always insisted that while faith and works, love
and justice are demanded of man, the commitment to the Law
is indispensable.

"Would that they forsook me and kept my law" (T.J.
Hagigah 1:7 and Midrash Rabbah on Lamentations Proem
2) said a rabbinic commentator of the will of the Lord.
Judaism has always contended that *how* a man lived was at

[5] "The evil inclination (yetzer) has no power over against the Law,
and he who has the Law in his heart over him the Yetzer has no power
(Midrash Psalms on 119:10).

"The words of the Law give life in this world and life in the world
to come" (Canticles Rabbah on 1:1).

least as important as what he claimed to believe, his action the test of his profession, his deed the sign of his intention. We have insisted that a man becomes what he does. Even if he comes to the service of the Righteous One for ulterior motives, his persistence in works of righteousness may lead him at last to the God of righteousness.

Properly understood, Torah is no less a method for achieving at-oneness with God than faith. Indeed in the paradoxical mystique of religion, both the law and belief are gifts of love from God, and both the man and his works must stand under the judgment of the Lord. What is given by creation needs to be offered back to God, transformed, enriched, completed, touched by human effort and striving. In this way, man remains eternally in dialogue with his Maker.

Even the Christian commentators who contend that law makes for sin and that faith alone frees, even these commentators are obliged in the end to restate the value of law. Even in a fellowship of allegedly "saved" men there is need for law in order to maintain balance among the conflicting goods towards which these men dedicate their lives.

Judaism asserts that society is yet unredeemed. Men can and do commit crimes; they are often brutal towards each other; even the faithful will interpret the word of the Lord differently and quarrel about it, sometimes violently. We can count neither on the goodness in men's hearts nor in the saving quality of their faith to achieve justice in society. There must be law and there must be courts—there must be a legislative agency and some recourse to a higher judicial authority. Good law helps man to sanctify life and society. Good government is a blessing.

Needless to say, law can be manipulated to perpetrate evil, government can be despotic and tyrannical. For that reason, in Judaism, law itself stands under the judgment of God. Kings and princes are as equally bound to His word as the peasant and pauper—all creation is under the authority of the Divine Presence.

In view of all this, then, we cannot accept Paul's presumption that the gentile can inherit the vocation of Abraham, namely, become Israel, without the yoke of Torah or the discipline of the Law.[6]

Israel

Man cannot and does not stand alone in this world. Individual redemption according to Jewish tradition, does not exist apart from the redemption of society. Man cannot be completely man without involvement in, relationship to, concern for his brother. Yet we know that each man must alone make his own choices in life. Each man must himself love God and choose life. We experience God's presence in our relationship with other human beings but God addresses us also individually.

Both understandings of God's relation to man appear in the Biblical text. These concepts are not contradictory—they are both paradoxically true. Man is individual but he is also part of society. Man will be fulfilled, will achieve Sholom, only when both aspects of his being are harmonized, completed, made one, whole—a promise for the end of time.

Judaism has always insisted that God's covenant is both with man and with a people. Fidelity to the Jewish people, therefore, is also part of our mission; for it will be the duty of

[6] "Were it not for the Book of the Law which was bequeathed to them, Israel would not have differed at all from the nations of the world" (Sifra 112c).

the people to achieve to God's kingdom through the establishment of a just society. There is evil in this world that partakes of a corporate nature and can only be resolved in a collective action. There are benefits for man to be derived by a just society and achieving it calls for human cooperation.

Each man will be judged according to his own deeds yet the Biblical mind knows also that the evils of our society visit their consequences even upon the third and fourth generation.[7]

Jewish tradition therefore looks upon peoplehood as a central feature of our mission. We are a holy nation. We cannot fulfill God's word unless, as a people, we can create a society, establish institutions, organize the appurtenances of a state. We must assume responsibility for the fashioning of a just government. That is why the establishment of the State of Israel takes on such religious significance for Jews.

It is true that the state came into being during the recent period of nationalistic revival and much of its building represents a response to a secular spirit. There were even some Jews who foolishly hoped that by achieving the "normalcy" of a national existence, by becoming like other nations, they could throw off the burden of their chosenness. It is also true that the state served a pragmatic and necessary function as haven for the bewildered refugees of Hitler who were welcomed in few other civilized nations.

---

[7] The Bible warns that God will visit "the iniquities of the fathers upon the children and the children's children to the third and fourth generation" (Exodus 20:5, 34:6); it promises that God "Keeps covenant and steadfast love with those who love Him and keep His commandments to a thousand generations" (Deuteronomy 7:9); but it also affirms "the soul that sins shall die" (Ezekiel 18:4). ". . . I will judge you, O House of Israel, everyone according to his ways. . . ." (Ezekiel 18:30).

But from the Jewish religious perspective, the establishment of the state takes on meaning only as the state itself and the society created within that state serve the purposes of God. The return to Zion and the rebuilding of Jerusalem are intertwined with Jewish Messianic aspirations.[8]

Most Jews who visit the modern State of Israel, even those who are religiously skeptic, cannot help but be touched with emotions of awe as they view the life that has sprouted forth from Palestine's wasteland. The tattooed wrecks of the concentration camps, the escapees from Communism, the oppressed, underprivileged denizens of the Jewish quarters of Islamic lands—these are the dead bones who bring new hope, new freedom to that beleagured land in the Middle East. There Jews once again, as the majority of the country, will be challenged to translate a Jewish vision of God's purpose into the living instrumentalities of government, law, and culture.

Those Jews who have found haven in other lands and take pride in their citizenship as Americans, Englishmen, Danes, Frenchmen, Italians, Germans, Dutch, Norwegians, and so forth, shall, through their various community relations organizations and synagogues, contribute as well to the fashioning of a just democratic society wherever they are.[9]

We shall also speak truth to our brothers in Israel and

[8] On that day when the Lord will bring us home and gather us together and make us renowned and praised among all the peoples of the earth (Zephaniah 3:20), on that day God promises also that He will cut off the battle bow and command peace to the nations. His dominions shall be from sea to sea and from the river to the ends of the earth (Zechariah 9:10). "And the Lord will become king over all the earth. On that day the Lord will be one and His name one" (Zechariah 14:9).

[9] "God scattered His people over the earth, for only so could all the nations be gained for His service" (Pesahim 87b).

criticize them when we believe that they have failed to live up to the highest potentiality of the Jewish faith. Even now, at this moment, Jews quarrel among themselves in every corner of the world. How shall Israel deal with missionaries, with its Christian and Islamic Arabs? What is the proper relation of a secular state to the Jewish religion? How Jewish can Israel be in fairness to its minority population? Where should Israel stand in the East-West struggle or in relation to the new African nationalities in conflict with Western colonial powers? To what degree should Israel seek security through military might or depend on the resources of an international community?

The struggle in Israel to define justice, to convert power into an agency of morality, to build a society, will reflect for good or ill upon the wisdom of the Jewish people.

Our faith compels us to be in and of the world, to work at it and with it. There is no genuine distinction between the secular and the holy. All is of God and is under God's judgment. Our task is to sanctify life by dedicating it completely, all of it, to His will. For that reason, we insist that we relate to God not only in our individuality but as a people in covenant.

We understand now the significance of the concept—"a kingdom of priests," a paradox in its own right since kingship matters of state, and the priesthood matters of God, are not coidentical realms. Jewish tradition rebuked the High Priests who wore the mantle of kingship; it insisted on the separation of function between church and state (Zechariah 4:1–4, 6:12 –13). Yet the necessary intermingling of religion and society is expressed by the Jewish conception of its own mission and self-identity as a kingdom of priests; and a holy nation—a nation that is obliged even in its most secular function to be open to the sanctifying nature of the Word.

We cannot agree with Paul's teaching that the Greek can become like the Jew, "Abraham's offspring," through "baptism into Christ" (Galations 3:27–29). The rabbis were correct to see in Paul's theology a danger to the Jewish faith, for our collectivity in the flesh is intended to serve and to fulfill our religious mission. Paul's teachings denied the Jewish conception of peoplehood. We acknowledge that the Greeks are of God and that God's law and purpose is for all men. Jews have long recognized that monotheists, Christian and Muslim, serve as witnesses to God and are to be praised for their success in converting masses of gentiles.[10] We ought even respect Paul's intention to expand the concept of the covenant in order to include pagans and idolaters within the faith of Abraham. But only we are Israel.

Olom Ha-Ba

As I have clearly indicated, we do not assert our mission with any spirit of arrogance. Our chosen-ness is indeed a burden. Rabbi Simeon Ben Yohai used to say: "Chastisements are precious. The Holy One, blessed be He, gave three gifts to Israel which the nations of the world desire and He gave them to Israel only through chastisements. They are Torah, the land of Israel, and the world to come" (Sifre on Deuteronomy 36:5).

The prophets on several occasions rebuked Israel by point-

[10] ". . . All the words of Jesus the Nazarene and of Mohammed who arose after him, came into being, only in order to make straight the road for the king Messiah, who will perfect the world enabling men to serve God together, as it is said, 'Then I shall turn all the peoples to a clear speech, that they may all call upon the Lord and serve Him shoulder to shoulder'" (Maimonides Mishneh Torah, Hilchot Melachim 11:4).

ing to the fidelity with which other nations served their Gods. In the profoundest, most universalistic conception of religion, a place in the world to come is assured all men who seek after righteousness.

Whereas Israel is called upon as the priest people to observe the *full* discipline of Torah, other nations by observance of the Noahide laws[11] are promised a share in the redemption. The righteous among the nations of the world are beloved of God.[12]

For this reason, therefore, Jews do not believe that they must convert others and bring them into the Jewish peoplehood in order to achieve the redemption of humankind. Let each nation, each people, all religions, come to God, each in their own way (Micah 4:5). If only they will be faithful to that which is *True* in their revelation, then we can hope that despite differences, men will live together in love and work together for justice.

[11] Even before the rabbinic period Jews believed that Noah, who was not a Hebrew, had enjoined upon his sons' sons a code of conduct, according to the will of God, binding upon all men (Jubilees 7:22). As elaborated in the Talmud (Tosephta Abodah Zarah 8:4–8, Sanhedrin 56a–60a), all human beings by virtue of their humanity are commanded to observe at least seven fundamental and religious principles proscribing: (1) idolatry; (2) adultery and incest; (3) bloodshed; (4) blasphemy; (5) robbery; (6) social injustice; (7) eating flesh cut from a living animal (inhuman treatment of animals). All non-Jews who observe these laws will participate in salvation and in the rewards of the world to come (Sanhedrin 105a). Some scholars believe that Paul acknowledges these basic natural laws (cf. Acts 15:20, 29).

[12] A rabbinic interpretation of the text "The Lord loveth the righteous: (Psalm 146:8)explains, "The Holy One blessed be He, says: 'They love Me and I love them also.' And why does the Holy One blessed be He, love the righteous? Because their righteousness is not a matter of heritage or family.

"May we not be like the lines which run parallel to each other," prayed a pious rabbi of the 17th century, "but rather like lines that enter the circle at different points and meet there in the center."

Jew and Gentile, Jews and Christians and Muslim, the slave and the free, men and women, all are under obligation to serve God and to work toward the redemption.[13]

But we do not believe that the Messiah has yet come even once. Judaism holds to many conceptions of what it will be like when the Messiah comes (or as the liberals say, "in the Messianic Era"). Some refuse to speculate; Maimonides, (Yad Melachim 12:1, 4f.) suggests that there will be no difference between our world and the days of the Messiah, except that man will be free of physical need or the threat of national servitude (and even these appear far off in achievment); others describe the world-to-come as a time when

---

"He will find that the priests form a father's house and the Levites form a father's house for it is said: 'O House of Aaron, Bless ye the Lord; O House of Levi, Bless ye the Lord' (Psalm 135:19–20). A man may wish to become a priest and yet he cannot. He may wish to become a Levite and yet he cannot, and why? Because his father was no priest or no Levite.

"But if a man, Jew or Gentile, wishes to be righteous, he can be this because the righteous do not form a house. Therefore, it is said, 'ye that fear the Lord, Bless ye the Lord' (Psalm 135:20). It is not said, *house* of those that fear the Lord, but *ye* that fear the Lord, for they form no father's house.

"Of their own free will, they came forward and loved the Holy One, blessed be He, and that is why He loves them" (Numbers Rabbah 8:2).

Although a righteous non-Jew is not a Jew, the rabbis expressed their conviction that even a gentile who engages in Torah, (namely, in works of righteousness), is like a High Priest (Abodah Zarah 3A).

[13] "The goal of wisdom is repentance and good works. So that a man may not study the Torah and learn the tradition and then set foot on

there will be no eating or drinking, no procreation of children or business, no envy or hatred or competition but the righteous sit, their crowns on the heads, and enjoy the splendor of the Divine Presence (Berachot 34B and 17A).

Clearly, at any rate, we do not see in our time any evidence of messianic fulfillment in natural or supernatural terms. Every step forward in civilization has brought man new blessings and greater fear. In Germany, Europe's most civilized and cultured country, murder erupted. In the heart of Catholic Italy, fascism reared its head. In the land of Orthodox splendor, Communism stands as judgment on Christian failure to achieve justice. In America's secular democracy men are losing a sense of purpose and meaning. The mind penetrates the mysteries of the universe only to place men under the anxiety of total annihilation.

Jews await that moment when all of history will be justified —even as we are aware that every moment, every time, provides an occasion, an opportunity for every individual to achieve a nearness to God. According to one rabbinic tradition, the Messiah is already here among us in this world, "sitting among poor lepers." Whereas others "unbind all their sores at once and then bind them up again, he unbinds one wound at a time and binds it up again straightaway thinking, should I perhaps be needed (to appear as the Messiah) I shall not be delayed" (Sanhedrin 98A).

Christians, too, struggle with the meaning of the redemp-

---

his brother or his mother or his master or on him who is greater than he in wisdom and in rank, thus it is said, 'the fear of the Lord is the beginning of wisdom; a good understanding have all they that do thereafter' " (Berachot 63B).

"I call heaven and earth to witness, that whether one be gentile or Jew, man or woman, slave or free man, the divine spirit rests on each in accordance with his *deeds*" (Tanhuma debe Eliyahu p. 48).

tion promised and given by faith in Jesus as the Christ. Some believe that once a Christian experiences rebirth he cannot fall from the grace. Others suggest that those in grace are given the power to grow toward perfection but that they must continually make confession and seek atonement for they will have fallen short. It is presumptuous of me here, as at other points in this address to attempt to define Christian doctrine —that will be your task. What it is that I can say, however, is that Jews believe that man can and does fulfill his responsibility to God by living as creatively and as righteously and as sanctified a life as possible here and now in this world. In His own time, God will save mankind with an everlasting salvation (Isaiah 45:17).

"Rabban Johanan Ben Zaccai used to say, 'If there be a plant in your hand when they say to you, behold the Messiah, go and plant the plant and afterward go out and greet him'" (Abot De Rav Nathan 31).

THE NEWNESS OF THE PRESENT ERA

My source texts are Biblical and rabbinic. They are ancient. Do they make sense in our fast-changing, dynamic, challenging world? You asked me to address you on the Jewish mission in history *and* in the modern world. Obviously, I have indicated my bias. I am Biblically-rooted and cannot conceive of Israel and our mission in any other terms. Not so, however, with all Jews.

One of the phenomena of our time is the degree of secularism that pervades our world; it has made its impact in the Jewish community. This is true for many reasons: Among them, the fact that democracy in Western civilization was in part the flowering of a humanistic, secularistic, liberal breakthrough from the narrowness and the confines of an authoritarian and feudal Christian church-statism. Jews have been granted a greater measure of freedom and respect under secular government than they ever received when the church ruled. Another factor is the reality that in a pluralistic world, in a world that is also decreasing in size but growing complex in technology, the role of organized religion seems to have diminished. Confronted by the onslaught of a scientific age, the fast movements of people and the growth of heterogeneity, the church and synagogue have retreated within their sanctuaries.

But the truth is that God is there in that world. We must become part of it. We must open our church windows so that holy incense may intermingle with factory smells and the odor of slums and the breath of perfume.

There are many Jews who are not part of the synagogue but they are Jews nevertheless. They define themselves in countless ways, yet no matter how they define themselves, they recognize that they are part of a people and they are loyal to that people. The sociologists inform us that even while observance of religious rituals appears to be declining among Jews, demonstrations of their associational loyalty to the Jewish people increases. (Christians who believe that lack of synagogue affiliation makes a Jew ripe for conversion, do not know us.)

Jewish religious leaders, of course, pray that all the Jewish people will recognize their responsibilities as a *holy* people; but what the religious leaders must also recognize is that there is holiness in the work of philanthropy, in the quest for racial justice, in the concern for peace that characterizes much of the life of Jews who are not in the synagogue.

Jews offer the world a conception of religion that demonstrates that it is not only a matter of affirming a creed, or joining a church, or regular prayer or Bible study, or having a faith, but it is also love of neighbor, the feeding of the poor, the clothing of the naked, the provision of shelter for the homeless. We offer a solution to the problem of secularity that can avoid the defensiveness reflected in the culture-religions of Western civilization.[14]

Jews offer the world also an understanding of how one can both at the same time hold to the uniqueness, the particular redemptive character of his own Vision, and still: *respect the dignity of the other*—an obligation, since man is a creation of the divine: *and cherish freedom of conscience*—for only in freedom can a man accept the yoke of kingdom; *and believe that there is truth nurtured in the other's revelation*—since God, Author of all History, speaks to men and nations through other human instrumentalities.

Jews and Christians differ, each in his conception of himself and both in a conception of the other. Yet there is much that we do share together, for the Jewish Testament after all is part of your heritage. There is much that we can and should do together to repair this world. In fact, if we do not lend our power to each other in cooperative effort to uproot evil and establish good, then we shall be deserving of God's sternest discipline.

[14] The rabbis taught: it is written "After the Lord, your God, shall ye walk" (Deuteronomy 13:5). They asked, what does this mean? Is it possible for man to walk after the presence of God? They answered, (not that man must pray three times daily, but rather), what it means is that we shall walk after the attributes of the Holy One blessed be He. He clothed the naked (Genesis 3:21). He visited the sick (Genesis 18:1). He comforted those who mourned (Genesis 25:11). He buried the dead (Deuteronomy 34:6). The Torah begins with the showing of mercy and it ends with the showing of mercy. Do likewise" (Sifre Deuteronomy 85A and Sotah 14A).

There is a rabbinic account of the rivalry between the schools of Hillel and Shammai. I would like to apply these words as well to all religious who differ with each other in good conscience:

> The words of *both* schools are the *words of the Living God.* But the law follows the ruling of the school of Hillel because they were gentle and modest, and studied both their own opinions and the opinions of the other school and humbly mentioned the words of the other school before theirs.
>
> This preference accorded to the school of Hillel teaches you that he who humbles himself, the Lord raises up; and he who exalts himself the Lord humbles. Greatness flees him who seeks greatness; greatness may follow him who flees from greatness. He who tries to force his hour is thrown back by time; he who yields to time finds his hour standing by him (Erubin 13B).

A POSTSCRIPT

If God were speaking to us out of our differences, if the fact of our separateness is of the will of God, if religious pluralism is a condition that seems permanent, what is it that He might be saying to us? What is His word for us as Jews and as Christians in our relation to each other, in a world that also includes pagans and secularists and atheists?

Permit me to point out that Judaism allows for religious pluralism and does not consider it scandalous. We suggest that God's plan for history might well be served were all peoples, however they worship their gods, to agree at least on a basic code of ethical principles, or on a procedure for living together that would enable men to provide cooperatively for the basic needs of humankind and assure themselves against the threat of physical annihilation. We do not believe that God's plan for salvation requires your conversion to Judaism nor mine to Christianity. But it does require our cooperation, our concern for, our joint effort to repair the world.

Beyond agreement on a modern reformulation of the "Noahide laws," Judaism will remain particularly committed to a vision of the God of Abraham that will challenge us always to achieve new and modern understanding of the "redemption from slavery." We are committed also to uproot idolatry—in all its modern manifestations: Military and political power, statism, materialism, nihilism.

We must even avoid the deification of religious organizations and the final formulation of our concepts of God, because beyond it lies the Living God, commanding us to do justice, love mercy, and walk humbly in His way. We shall minister to the nations and witness to the living God, not with the outmoded methods of proselytizing, but rather by the sacrificial example of dedicated lives. Our existence as Jews must speak powerfully to mankind. All the manipulative methods of modern-day advertising and mass media communications are ineffectual in comparison to the life of Abraham.

We remain aware also that God's revelation is continual. He reveals himself not to Israel alone, but to all men and nations; and if we open our hearts we shall find Him in history speaking to us through committed Christians, in the striving of the black African for dignity, out of the pain of the disfigured of Hiroshima, in the cry of the Hungarian refugee, and through many others who inherit this earth.

There are important lessons Jews can learn from the Christian: Christianity once addressed the outcast and dispossessed with a sensitivity that surpassed the charity of the organized synagogue. Today church and synagogue are challenged by problems of racial discrimination and human poverty. We must measure up to our convictions or face God's judgment upon our institutions.

Christianity with its emphasis on individual salvation provided hope to those who had suffered outrageously in the processes of group living, or who had been overcome by despair at the difficulty of achieving any sense of at-oneness with God so long as society remained shockingly corrupt and chaotic. Today God still offers His peace to those who come to Him; although once unburdened the believer must join himself to a fellowship of faithful, if faith is to be translated into life-serving energy.

Christianity, despite a suspect history of inter-creedal violence, has inspired "Peace churches" whose followers have demonstrated that methods of peace, nonviolent resistance, and self-sacrifice are effective means for healing such disorders of humankind as suspicion, hate, vengeance, violence, and war. Today in an age of thermonuclear destruction and explosive group conflict we had better recapture that vision or perish.

Christianity, in its concern for the world universal, spoke a corrective word to a Hebraic tendency to tribalism. It enlarged the narrow folk perspective that at times hemmed in the Jewish vision.

Above all, Christianity insists that it has remained faithful to the spiritual heritage of covenanted Israel. The church has attempted to enlarge the concept of Israel so as to include within it all of humanity, all who would believe in and hold fast to ideals and values communicated through the life of him whom they claim fulfilled the Jewish Law. Jews can not gainsay the fact that through this vision Christians have nurtured and preserved an appreciation for the God of Abraham. They have made it part of the heritage of our civilization. Their belief that Christ came and will appear again provides a vigorous assurance and a will-to-courage for all who await still the ultimate redemption of mankind. Indeed, their conviction even quickens the hearts of those of us in Israel who still await the Messiah. Together, we share a realization that life does have religious purpose, and that history affords us the occasion to demonstrate that God is one.

Judaism, on the other hand, challenges a "successful" Christian church, that has become identified with the idolatrous power of the state to recognize that church and state are not one, and that religion has a prophetic function that the church sacrifices only at the price of its integrity.

Jews teach a complacent church, too concerned with its institutional welfare, that the crucified Christ cannot be confined to the church. Rather He is with all those who suffer because of the sins of mankind. Jews have borne the penalties of Christian apostasy from their Christ. The prototype of the suffering servant in contemporary history has been the Jewish people.

Judaism reminds Christians who distorted the doctrine of redemption, thinking that once they had achieved to a self-satisfying faith they were assured of salvation and needed no longer to concern themselves with the harsh affairs of this world, Judaism reminds these Christians that "to be a Jew (or a Christian) means a readiness to suffer crucifixion" (Shemot Rabbah 42:9). The quest for redemption necessarily must involve the believer in taking positions and making choices toward the resolution of all human problems on this earth. This responsibility leaves us only at death.

Judaism continues to remind Christianity of its own essential doctrine that God is known not by dogmas defined or redefined, reformed or counterreformed, but He is revealed in history when the Word becomes Event. The Jewish search for a *righteous act* is counterbalance to the Christian quest for a *unifying creed*.

The God of Abraham who is singular, who takes no human form or shape, who can never be fully defined, whom we are challenged to know as best we can in our hearts and also with our minds, that God stands in judgment over all human institutions, including church and synagogue.

In the paradox of religion, strength is our weakness, and our weakness is strength. Humbled, I suggest that God's *Truth* is larger than any of us have or could have encompassed. Conversing with each other we discover that God is among us revealing Himself anew.

The rabbis teach: "God reveals Himself to each man according to his strength" (Pesikta Rabbati Ch. 12). I conclude these unfinished words with the declaration recited at the end of the reading in the synagogue of each book of Torah—Chazak Chazak V'nitchazek—"Be strong, be strong, and may you be renewed in strength."